THE COSMOPOLITAN CHRISTIAN

Tomi Arayomi

What if the answer to wolves dressed as sheep
will be sheep dressed as wolves?

D1519281

Cosmopolitan Christian
1st Edition

Foreword

Are we, the body of Christ turning the world upside down like we should be today, or is the world turning us upside down instead?

The Cosmopolitan Christian is a timely book in which Tomi Arayomi sounds a clarion call that must be heeded with expediency. This is not an easy read for your flight to LA. Prepare to be stretched, stirred, and equipped to take action, for the church's most urgent yet finest hour lays straight ahead.

The church after all is not peripheral to the world, it is the other way around. The world is peripheral to the church through which Christ rules the universe (Ephesians 1:23 MSG).

Taking into account the chaos and darkness we find surrounding us today, we must look within the church to determine why we are not leading in influence. Have we lost our potency? Why aren't we winning over our cities, and discipling nations? Why aren't we shaping culture? Why aren't we demonstrating the power of our God with miracles, healings, signs and wonders?

The message within the pages of this book highlights distinctions in the Word that will help you recognize which spirit is in operation and how to respond biblically. Tomi also offers keen insights through his personal life story, helping the reader to discern when man-made rules have been cleverly disguised to masquerade themselves as God-given laws. Using Jesus as the prime example, we see that even though He never sinned, Jesus was the ultimate rule-breaker. To the consternation of the rule-enforcing Pharisees, He healed people on the Sabbath, touched lepers, and dined with sinners.

Finally, He who knew no sin bore the full weight of our sins upon Himself and absorbed every curse in order to free us from the demonic control of the sin-slave system. Talk about the ultimate breaking of rules, Satan never saw that one coming!

Christ revealed the highest law through His perfect redemption: "...the Law of the Spirit of life has set us free in Christ Jesus from the Law of sin and death" (Romans 8:2 Berean Literal). In the same way, He also shows us the highest culture, the culture of Heaven. Jesus explains, "The kingdom of heaven is like leaven that a woman took and hid in three measures of flour, till it was all leavened" (Matthew 13:33 ESV).

This leaven is Heaven's culture, and the woman who took and hid that leaven speaks of the church. When the Jesus people witnessed to me on the streets of LA, they began infusing me with the utterly irresistible culture of Heaven. Born and raised in communist Bulgaria, I was a brainwashed atheist and did not believe anything that they were saying to me. Yet as they shared with me each day that Jesus loved me and that He died for me, they were kind and patient. These Jesus people were demonstrating His love for me and placing His value into me. That higher culture soon began to disarm my defenses. Although my cultural norm was fear and mistrust, they managed to bypass all of that and befriend me. Ultimately this caused me to open my heart just enough to test out what they were saying. To my great surprise, I found myself falling into the nail-scarred hands of my loving Savior. I'll never forget my reaction, "Of course there is a God! The Communists lied to us about everything, they lied to us about God too!"

Now, back to the church. Using the lens that Tomi provides helps us discover clues of how the church loses its potency, and how true apostolic leaders can help restore it.

In Acts chapter two, the Holy Spirit came as a rushing mighty wind to the disciples in the upper room. They were engulfed in flames of fire and spoke in other tongues. The international crowd drawn in by the noise of the wind were all able to understand them in their own language. This supernatural phenomenon caused the church of Jesus Christ in Jerusalem to explode. Three thousand believers were birthed into the Kingdom that very day, and the Lord continued adding to their numbers daily.

By chapter twenty-one, we see that the church in the city grew into the tens of thousands. This is remarkable, yet there was a significant problem brewing. Even though they were growing in numbers, the church was losing their influence because they could not establish the full authority of Christ. The root cause became apparent when the apostle Paul returned to Jerusalem for a visit. Suddenly the city was stirred up because the Jerusalem Christians were upset that Paul was not minding the Mosaic laws.

Christ had fulfilled the law of Moses, but the church in Jerusalem was not quite ready to let go of their religious system and long held traditions. The blood of the Lamb had been poured out on the Cross, yet they continued with old ceremonial laws and the offering of sacrifices in the Temple (Acts 21:21). This undermined among them what Christ had accomplished and created a religious hybrid of sorts. The church had been birthed in freedom and power and now suddenly had its own set of man-made rules. Their re-packaged, re-branded version of the Gospel caused them to lose their savor and essence because they mixed the pure unadulterated grace of Christ with the law system of Moses.

Fortunately, the revelation that God gave to the Apostle Paul had not been corrupted. He was ministering outside of Jerusalem and turning the Gentile world upside down city by city. In Ephesus, their idolatrous industry was no longer making a profit because of the great number of Christian converts there (Acts 19). In Philippi, the city was shaken violently by Paul and Silas's prison worship session, helping to grow and establish the first European church that began in Lydia's house in signs and wonders (Acts 16). In Thessalonica, Paul and Silas stirred up the entire city by saying that Jesus is King and not Caesar (Acts 17:6-7), and in Athens, Paul boldly confronted the contemporary philosophers and thought leaders and made several new disciples out of them.

In three out of the four cities that I just mentioned, religious and political leaders stirred up mobs to incite riots in the streets because of Paul's preaching of the Gospel there. Paul and his companions were radical disruptors. What would we do today if Paul and Silas were disrupting cosmopolitan cities like London or New York like they did in the Bible? Would mob rule silence us? Would we be able to discern what is happening or would we repeat like parrots the latest media mantra?

These are the types of questions that you will find yourself asking out loud as you read the pages ahead. Tomi has the mind of a philosopher, the heart of a poet in love with His Savior, and the transparent spirit of a prophet. A Nigerian child raised in the United Kingdom by his African parents; he has also been able to make astute observations about all of the different cultural forces at play around him. This has given him the ability to recognize and synthesize vital life topics for today's believer and offer a strategic roadmap of hope for this generation. Well done Tomi!

Georgian Banov, President and Co-Founder, Global Celebration and GCSSM ONLINE, author, *Joy! God's Secret Weapon for Every Believer*
General Director of The Bulgarian Interlinear Bible Project
Chairman of the Bulgarian Spring of Life Foundation

Introduction

The Cosmopolitan Christian

Over the centuries we have seen dramatic advancements in the levels of revelation given to the church by the Spirit of God. These changes have been ushered in by believers who were beacons to their generation, endowed with supernatural abilities and heralded by many as pioneers or revivalists. When we think of great moves of God in Christianity, our minds can't help but gravitate towards people like the late great John G Lake and Kathryn Kuhlman, to name but a few. These were the John the Baptists of their day.

Every generation needs a John the Baptist to usher in a new movement. John is the entrée that signals the emergence of a new breed of Christ-follower.

> *"A voice of one calling in the wilderness, 'Prepare the way for the Lord, make straight paths for him.'"*
> *Mark 1:3 (NIV)*

John had fearless, prophetic conviction and, through bold and unpopular speech, prepared his generation for a new move of God, so that rejection of this fresh direction was minimised.

I was born in 1987 and gave my life to Jesus Christ at the age of fifteen. Over my eighteen years in ministry, I have become increasingly aware of a dramatic shift in my generation's thought process. This shift, unbeknownst to many in Christendom, marks the dawn of another awakening, but unfortunately there are few contemporary beacons of prophetic conviction signalling the ushering in of this movement through bold and unpopular speech.

My intention in writing this book is to leverage what reputation I have garnered over the years to give voice to this generation.

New paradigm

It has been said that every new move of God is doomed to encounter opposition from an old move of God. Whilst this can't be avoided, the damage can be mitigated. In writing this book, I intend to provide a pathway through the thicket so that generations to come may walk with the certitude and intentionality necessary to ride out the adversity and to redefine criticism from being an impediment or discouragement, but rather as being a measurement of success.

> *Blessed are those who have been persecuted for righteousness' sake, for theirs is the Kingdom of Heaven. Matthew 5:10 (WEB)*

Whilst statistics are unanimous that there is a worldwide exodus of young people from the values of their Christian predecessors, what if this Exodus is a parallel of the Exodus in the Scriptures and what if what we are witnessing as being a move away from something, Heaven is in fact witnessing as being a move towards something?

Global

I recently became interested in the word 'cosmopolitan' and decided to check the word out in my favourite dictionary Merriam-Webster. This is what it said:

cosmopolitan *adjective*
> *"Having WorldWide rather than limited or provincial (local) scope or bearing"*

Why is this important? Jesus instructs us to:

> *"Go into all the world and preach the gospel to all creation"*
> *Mark 16:15 (NIV)*

There is something in the hardwiring of today's young people that is causing them to have a worldwide rather than localised perspective. Technology has disrupted the next generation and has shifted its entire paradigm from the local viewpoint thought to global outlook. Social media apps have made the world smaller, more accessible and reachable. In the midst of a cosmopolitan world, God is already raising up an end time cosmopolitan church that does not compromise on its values, faith or power. Moreover, criticism will rise up against it because many will misconstrue 'covert' for 'compromise.'

One day, whilst I was sitting in my house, the Lord challenged me with a thought,

*What if the answer to wolves dressed as sheep will be
sheep dressed as wolves?*

This thought has formed the foundation for the writing of this
book. I want to show you how a local church can build a
global vision and how a local Christian can have a global
impact by being in the world and not of the world. The end goal
and final mission of this new breed, which I am dubbing the
Cosmopolitan Christian, will be:

*To make the kingdoms of the world the kingdom of our God
and of His Christ!
Revelation 11:15 (Paraphrased)*

Chapter One

The Kosmos
The fall that changed it all

The word 'cosmopolitan' comes from two Greek words, politês, meaning citizen, and *kosmos* from where we get the word *cosmos*, meaning world, world order, world system or universe.

A cosmopolitan person is a person of worldly smarts, savvy and possessing an international sophistication. That person is not easily beguiled because they have a worldwide, as opposed to a limited, provincial frame of reference.

We all know that Christianity is built on the foundation of moral absolutes which were first laid out in the Ten Commandments. We can also observe that these absolutes have alienated the church from the cosmopolitan community at large for which morality is relative and not absolute. This has been an insurmountable impasse for the Body of Christ.

God has called the church to go into a morally bankrupt *kosmos* that by and large is dramatically incongruent with our Christian way of life and, furthermore, seeks to eradicate Christianity entirely from its systems of thought, humanities, schools, governments and arts.

> *Why do the heathen rage, and the people imagine a vain thing? The kings of the earth set themselves, and the rulers take counsel together, against the Lord, and against his anointed, saying,*
> *Psalm 2:1-2 (KJV)*

Totally eradicating Jesus is the goal, along with setting up a form of morality based entirely on who can 'out virtue signal' the other person by a subjective standards of goodness or identity victimhood with no clear objective moral arbiter is the reason the Bible says,

> So where does this leave the philosophers, the scholars, and the world's brilliant debaters? God has made the wisdom of this world look foolish.
> 1 Corinthians 1:20 (NLT)

In the beginning...

To understand God's plan for the Kosmos, we must first understand the book of Genesis. In it, we find details to the origins of the world, though not as we now know it!

In Genesis Chapter 1, we see God creating mankind, in the image and likeness of God Himself. Let's be careful to not miss the hybridity of God's creation.

> Then God said, "Let us make mankind in our image, in our likeness, so that they may rule over the fish in the sea and the birds in the sky, over the livestock and all the wild animals, and over all the creatures that move along the ground."
> Genesis 1:26 (NIV)

The book of Genesis is a book of 'genes' (hence Genesis). It traces mankind's original DNA back to God and boldly contradicts modern day Darwinian thought. Darwinism states that man more or less evolved from a single-celled organism, whereas God's Word says man's DNA was pulled out of God Himself.

Our ancestry is indeed the most important part of the journey to becoming the cosmopolitan Christian because, if Darwin was right and his audacious rewrite of our genetic history is the foundation of our existence, then our morality and destiny should indeed be as random, selective and relative as our so-called incidental existence. By allowing Darwin and his apologist proponents to detrimentally downplay our existence, over time we have allowed the validity of the existence of the spirit, soul and purpose to be eroded.

However, if God's definition is true and we did not come about through natural selection, but rather through divine election, then our purpose in this cosmos is far more detailed and complex than we could have ever imagined possible.

God's account of our origin can be summed up in Genesis as the duplication of a perfect Heaven in an imperfect earth. The opening Scriptures say,

> "In the beginning God created the heavens and the earth. Now the earth was formless and empty, darkness was over the surface of the deep, and the Spirit of God was hovering over the waters."
> Genesis 1:1 (NIV)

God made Earth just like heaven. By simply saying, 'let', He established the Earth. The same 'let' was how Jesus taught His disciples to pray.

*"Let your Kingdom come. Let your will be done, on earth as
it is in heaven."*
Matthew 6:10 (NIV)

This letting allowed heaven to be planted in the earth or, as the
Book of Isaiah more elaborately describes it:

*That I may plant the heavens, and lay the foundations of
the earth...*
Isaiah 51:16 (KJV)

This planting of the heavens by God created a framework
made up of entirely spiritual matter. In Genesis 1, God was
intent on completing Creation through speaking it into being.
His Words had the ability to construct a spiritual skeleton
through which He could in Genesis 2.

The dawn of the kinds

*"Then God said, "Let the land produce vegetation: seed-
bearing plants and trees on the land that bear fruit with
seed in it, according to their various kinds." And it was so.."*
Genesis 1:11 (NIV)

Notice the word "kind". If prayer is speaking what is on Earth
as it is in Heaven, there is a perfect demonstration in Genesis
when God says 'according to their various kinds,' In other
words, the kinds that God created in Heaven, He reproduced
in the Earth (as it is in Heaven).

God made:

Plant kind - Genesis 1:11
Marine kind - Genesis 1:20
The terrestrial kind - Genesis 1:24
The insect kind - Genesis 1:24
God kind - Genesis 1:27

Notice that in this framework, God separated man from the animals. Why did he do this? It was because He made everything after its own kind in Heaven, hence, "according to its kind." However, when it came to the DNA of man, God created man after God Himself.

> *Then God said, "Let us make mankind in our image, in our likeness, so that they may rule over the fish in the sea and the birds in the sky, over the livestock and all the wild animals, and over all the creatures that move along the ground."*
> *Genesis 1:26 (NIV)*

God made mankind to be like god kind!

God is not a name!
The word 'God' in the Hebrew is Elohim. Its root word is 'El'. It literally means:

Ruler
Judge
Magistrate
Supreme

In order to understand a 'god' that creates beings in His image we have to first understand that 'God' is not a name!

Throughout Scripture we see others being given the name god.

Jesus in the book of John was accused by the Jews of blasphemy, stating

> We are not stoning you for any good work," they replied, "but for blasphemy, because you, a mere man, claim to be God."
> John 10:33 (NIV)

Jesus responded,

> "Is it not written in your Law, 'I have said you are "gods"
> John 10:34 (NIV)

In 2 Corinthians 4:4, Satan is referred to as

> "the god of this world".

In Exodus 7:1, Moses is referred to as

> "god to Pharaoh".

If 'God' was a name, then Lucifer would not have been called a god, Moses would not have been called a god and human beings like us would not have been called gods by Jesus.

In fact, the Bible goes on to say,

*And I appeared to Abraham, to Isaac, and to Jacob, as God
Almighty; but by my name Yahweh I was not known to
them.*
Exodus 6:3 (WEB)

Here, God is saying to Moses (paraphrasing), "God' is not My
name!'

Yahweh (The Lord) is His name. God is His office.

When the Bible speaks of Lucifer being a god, it is not
speaking of a name, it is speaking again of an office. This is
what the religious leaders could not understand and this again
is what many religious people misunderstand today.

The reason why the chief angels of Heaven are denoted by
'El', being the root word for 'god', at the end of their name is
because they all are/were rulers of their own interests.

> *Gabri EL (Gabriy'el)*
> *Micha EL (Miyka'el)*
> *Hal El (Heylel)* (Lucifer)

Lucifer is now the ruler, magistrate and judge of this
cosmopolitan world. If you would believe it, he always has
been! I will explain this in greater depth later.

God made Adam and Eve and it was their assignment to rule
Earth in treaty with Heaven, to dominate it as God dominates
heaven.

17

Then God said, "Let us make mankind in our image, in our likeness, so that they may rule over the fish in the sea and the birds in the sky, over the livestock and all the wild animals, and over all the creatures that move along the ground."
Genesis 1:26 (NIV)

Creation Vs Formation

In His image - Tselem
In Genesis 1:26, God created Adam as a bi-product of Himself. What exactly is God and what DNA did He use to make man that He did not use in the making of the other kinds?

> *God is spirit...*
> *John 4:24 (NIV)*

When God made man, He created a duplicate of His spirit or what Genesis 1:26 calls 'image' or '*tselem*' in the Hebrew, meaning phantom!

Genesis 1:26 is Adam's creation. It is what we call the 'god kind' in the mankind. Remember, Adam here is a god by office and not by worship. His job is to rule earth like God rules heaven!

Other variants of '*tselem*' help us to understand what God was doing.

> *1. Illusion - perception of something objectively existing in such a way as to cause misinterpretation of its actual nature.*

2. Phantom - Something apparent to the senses but with no substantial matter.
3. Shade - A disembodied spirit

So in Genesis 1, God did not create a body, but a spirit as a direct representative of Him.

For the LORD your God is God of gods and Lord of lords,
the great God, mighty and awesome
Deuteronomy 10:17 (NIV)

In His likeness - demuth

Adam although in the image of God in Genesis 1, was not made in the likeness of God until Genesis 2.

Likeness is the Hebrew word, *demuth,* it means:

1. *Likeness - Appearance*
2. *Similitude - A visible likeness or an imaginative comparison*
3. *Model - A miniature representation of something*
4. *Concrete - to form into a solid mass*
5. *Fashion - The make or form of something*

Adam was created in Genesis 1, but concreted in Genesis 2!

*Then the LORD God **FORMED** a man from the dust of the ground and breathed into his nostrils the breath of life, and the man became a living being.*
Genesis 2:7

In Genesis 1, a god (little-g) is created and blessed! In Genesis 2, a man is formed.

What is even more interesting about this is that God takes the insubstantial creation and substantiates it by making it of the very cosmological elements that it is called to rule - *the dust!*

This means that the Genesis-1-Adam is in the image of God= god and the Genesis-2-Adam is in the image of earth=man.

> *Genesis 1 is made in the image of God.*
> *Genesis 2 is made in the image of the earth.*

Both are the same Adam, just that Genesis 1 is His creation and Genesis 2 is His formation.

> *As we have borne the image of those made of dust, let's*
> *also bear the image of the heavenly.*
> *1 Corinthians 15:49 (WEB)*

Adam is a god kind of man! A hybrid of sorts, with two images. One being His true image and the other being what I call 'the redemptive quality'.

'God' or 'ruler' was his creation and dust was his formation. Understanding the creation/formation differences give greater insight into what God meant in Jeremiah chapter 1 when He said,

> *"Before I **FORMED** you in the womb I knew you, before*
> *you were born I set you apart; I appointed you as a prophet*
> *to the nations."*
> *Jeremiah 1:5 (NIV)*

Chapter Two

Parallel Dimensions
The Story of the Dual Citizen

Story Time

I was born in Ibadan, Nigeria on 7th January 1987. My parents emigrated to Scotland in the United Kingdom in 1989. I was two years old when we arrived in Glasgow. They worked hard and were eventually naturalized in the United Kingdom. My dad is now a medical doctor and consultant in Essex, United Kingdom. My mum become a successful dentist with her own dental practice, also in Essex.

We were naturalised after living many years in the United Kingdom. I now possess both a Nigerian passport and a United Kingdom passport. This means I am 100% Nigerian and 100% British at the same time. I am a dual citizen entitled to the same privileges in both countries as any other citizen.

Whilst the process of naturalisation is quite complex, the principles are simple. I have a document with an image on it called a passport. I am not allowed entry into the Country or to *'pass the portal'* (passport) unless the image on the document aligns with the image standing before the customs officer.

I was not born in the United Kingdom, I was born in Nigeria, but I was formed in the United Kingdom. I hope by now you are beginning to see where I am going with this story.

I knew you before you knew you!

> "Before I **FORMED** you in the womb I knew you, before
> you were born I set you apart; I appointed you as a prophet
> to the nations."
> Jeremiah 1:5 (NIV)

How is it remotely possible that the Lord knew me before I
knew me? David goes a step further in the Book of Psalms
and says:

> Your eyes saw my un**FORMED** substance; in your book
> were written, every one of them, the days that were formed
> for me, when as yet there was none of them.
> Psalm 139:16 (ESV)

If what David says is true and there was a 'me' before there
was a 'me'? What I now identify as 'self', God says is simply a
formed (redemptive) part of me. There was an unformed part
of me, a prophet, fully existing, but not made of the same
matter as the other kinds! This matter made me special,
unique and set me apart from all the other beasts of the earth.
My form is merely illusory and a simile of who I really am.

> Listen to me, distant nations, you people who live far away!
> **BEFORE I WAS BORN**, the LORD chose me and
> appointed me to be his servant.
> Isaiah 49:1 (GNT)

Understanding the story of Genesis is pivotal to our stance as
Christians in a world that is so hostile to Christianity today. It is
the reason I believe that Genesis is the first book of the Bible.

It is the reason why secular education has so aggressively sought to change our image and indoctrinate the masses through Darwinian theories trafficked as fact. My brother Tobi Arayomi's theory is that the devil conceived a plan to deceive the masses that if he could convince man that we came from apes then one day we would act like monkeys. If the enemy could remove the image of God from our viewpoint, he could rewrite our entire history and indeed our future as he is doing today.

> *In whom the god of this world (Lucifer) has blinded the minds of the unbelieving, that the light of the Good News of the glory of Christ, who is the image of God, should not dawn on them.*
> *2 Corinthians 4:4 (WEB)*

Where is Heaven?

Heaven is in earth, or rather, I should say earth is in Heaven. The two worlds are not worlds apart as we might presume. In actual fact, when Lucifer fell from heaven, he told us where Heaven was latitudinally

> *For you said to yourself, 'I will ascend to heaven and set my throne above God's stars. I will preside on the mountain of the gods far away in the north. Isaiah 14:13 (NIV)*

Heaven is north of our location and is far away. Just how far exactly? We don't know! Isaiah just says it's high up there beyond the cosmos!

> *As the heavens are higher than the earth, so are my ways higher than your ways and my thoughts than your thoughts.*

Isaiah 55:9 (NIV)

Although locationally Heaven is far above the earth, jurisdictionally Heaven is in the Earth or Earth is in the Heavens. When a nation's ambassador comes into another nation, it is as good as one kingdom being in another.

Jesus, the ambassador of Heaven came into the Earth and said although the Kingdom is locationally far away, it is here because I am here.

> *The kingdom of Heaven is at hand.*
> *Matthew 4:17 (WEB)*

We will talk about this in the chapter titled, 'Kingdom versus Kosmos', but for now it is important to know that God created the Earth to mirror Heaven. In fact, Heaven is a parallel dimension of Earth and whatever God makes on earth, He makes it 'as it is in heaven.'

This is why the Disciples ask Jesus to teach them how to pray. Prayer is asking God to reproduce heaven in earth just as it is in heaven.

> *Your kingdom come, your will be done, on earth as it is in heaven.*
> *Matthew 6:10 (NIV)*

When your prayers are not answered, it is for two reasons.
- You are not asking

- You are asking God to do something on earth that He has not already established in heaven. This is what it means to ask amiss.

Ye have not, because ye ask not. Ye ask, and receive not, because ye ask amiss
James 4:2-3 (KJV)

God is looking to us in this hour to learn to be the master asker. In order for Kingdom to invade the Kosmos (world) we must learn to ask according to what is already in heaven, the parallel universe that earth was created to mirror. No man-made system lasts that is not already established in heaven! God's Kingdom is everlasting and so, in order for us to have lasting legacy, we must learn to build what is already in Heaven on Earth – meaning as it is, and not less than it is in Heaven.

*I will give to you the keys of the Kingdom of Heaven, and whatever you bind on earth **WILL HAVE BEEN BOUND IN HEAVEN**; and whatever you release on earth **WILL HAVE BEEN RELEASED IN HEAVEN.**"*
Matthew 16:19 (WEB)

Again, we will talk about this more in the chapter titled 'Kingdom vs Kosmos.' For now, it is important to understand this foundational truth that Earth was made in the mirror or reflection of Heaven to exact detail.

Adam, as a dual citizen, would have seen the natural world from the spiritual world. His job, was to ensure that the two worlds align and that the treaty between the two worlds was sustained. As a consequence of his fall, we now see into that spirit (mirrored) world only very dimly and without great clarity.

For now we see in a mirror, dimly
1 Corinthians 13:12 (NASB)

When God was finding the *'kinds'* written about in chapter one, He was sourcing them from the *'kinds'* in Heaven. So, if you ever want to know what Heaven looks like, it looks like a more glorified form of Earth. Everything on earth is a copy and mere shadow of their true heavenly existence.

Who serve a copy and shadow of the heavenly things
Hebrews 8:5 (NASB)

The Mirror World

God lives in a dimensionally, transcendent and morally diametrically opposed world outside of our three dimensions. This means that just as you cannot get there simply by public transport, you cannot reason His existence within the moral framework of your own. His world is just as real as our own. In fact, His world is the causal world and our world is the effect world. Everything that happens in our world is a mere shadow of everything that has already happened in the spirit world. Our world works forward, His world works backwards.

For example, in our world Jesus was slain 2000+ years ago, but in God's world, Jesus was slain from the foundation of the Earth. In essence, to the Omniscient God, Jesus died in Genesis.

…the Lamb who was slain from the creation of the world.

27

Revelation 13:8 (NIV)

We see life from the beginning to the end, God sees life from the end to the beginning. This is why God is never worried about the things that worry us.

> *I am God, and there is none like me.* ***I MAKE KNOWN THE END FROM THE BEGINNING****, from ancient times, what is still to come. I say, 'My purpose will stand, and I will do all that I please.'*
> *Isaiah 46:9-10 (KJV)*

God is omnipresent meaning that He is trans-locational. Because time is not linear in Heaven, but constant and eternal, God can sit in the beginning of your life, the end of your life and the pre-beginning of your life all at the same time.

> *"I am the Alpha and the Omega," says the Lord God, "who is, and who was, and who is to come, the Almighty."*
> *Revelation 1:8 (NIV)*

God is both beginning and ending simultaneously. (Is this hurting your head yet?) This is why in our eyes, our life began at conception but in God's eyes (who was), your life began long before conception.

Purpose is not about discovery, purpose is about recovery!

Earthen Vessels

When God said to Jeremiah that He knew him before he was formed, is it possible that God was speaking about Jeremiah's spirit-(unformed substance, the part made as god and from the Most High God)?

The unformed substance or spirit is called to rule with God. However, God seems to wrap this treasure in dirt! Why?

> *But we have this treasure in earthen vessels, that the*
> *excellency of the power may be of God, and not of us.*
> *2 Corinthians 4:7 (KJV)*

God put your spirit in an air tight clay vessel made of dirt from the very ground He has called your spirit to rule over because He doesn't want the air to get to your head and for you to think that the success of your life was gained through your strength.

God put Adam's spirit in the very dirt He called Him to rule over! He put dirt around greatness so that greatness will never forget where it came from and Who it came from!

> *For dust you are and to dust you will return.*
> *Genesis 3:19 (NIV)*

God made Adam and Eve and it was their assignment to rule Earth in treaty with Heaven, to dominate it as God dominates heaven.

> *Then God said, "Let us make mankind in our image, in our*
> *likeness, so that they may rule over the fish in the sea and*
> *the birds in the sky, over the livestock and all the wild*
> *animals, and over all the creatures that move along the*
> *ground."*
> *Genesis 1:26 (NIV)*

In Adam, God made a god. He wrapped him in a man and placed the man in a garden to keep it. In other words, God conditioned the man in the spirit, but positioned the man in the cosmological system. He gave the man the job of cultivating the earth. Without a body, there can be no cultivation.

The word cultivate means to culture. The Genesis 2, Adam was formed to re-culture the Earth from the dimension of Genesis 1.

'Aram'

The Genesis 2 man was not aware that he was a Genesis 2 man because, whilst He existed in Genesis 2, he lived entirely in Genesis 1.

> *Although both the man and his wife were naked, they were not ashamed.*
> *Genesis 2:25 (CEV)*

Adam and Eve were so immersed in their divinity that they had no idea that they were also human beings. Their senses were fully locked into their heavenly, unformed and unsubstantiated state (spirit) that they had no idea that they were naked or indeed flesh.

The word for 'naked' is an interesting word. It is taken from the root word in the Hebrew, '*aram'*, meaning shrewd, crafty and cunning. It is very different from the word naked used when it later describes Adam and Eve as beholding that they were naked (Genesis 3:7.) The former describes Adam and Eve as somehow cunningly concealed, as if God wanted their true essence to be intentionally underestimated by the onlooker.

> *But one in a certain place testified, saying, What is man,*
> *that thou art mindful of him? or the son of man, that thou*
> *visitest him?*
> *Hebrews 2:6 (KJV)*

Ever more interesting is that this word 'aram' is the same root word used to describe Satan in Genesis 3:1.

> *Now the serpent was more crafty than any beast of*
> *the field which the LORD God had made. And he said*
> *to the woman, "Indeed, has God said, 'You shall not*
> *eat from any tree of the garden'?"*
> *Genesis 3:1 NASB*

Satan came disguised as a snake and god came disguised as a man. Man is not how you were born, man is how you were formed (Genesis 2:7)! You were born a spirit, but you were formed a man. Satan was born a spirit, but formed as a snake. The serpent was a part of God's creation that surrendered itself over to Satan to deceitfully con Adam out of his possession.

Yatsar

See the Hebrew word for 'formed' below:

> *Original Word:* יָצַר
> *Part of Speech: Verb*
> *Transliteration: yatsar*

Phonetic Spelling: (yaw-tsar')
Short Definition: formed or to fashion

The body is the fashion of the spirit! It is designed to craftily conceal you and not necessarily to protect you, otherwise it would not be so fragile! The body was not made for protection, but for concealment.

This is why Jesus came in a body! It was a crafty concealment of His true identity! This is why Paul says,

> *None of the rulers of this age understood it, for if they had,*
> *they would not have crucified the Lord of glory.*
> *1 Corinthians 2:8 (NIV)*

God concealed Himself in man and Lucifer concealed himself in serpent.

Adam and Eve fell because Satan managed to convince Eve that she was nothing more than flesh and if she were to take the fruit, she would be who she in fact already was. Instead of becoming like God (who she already was like) her and Adam became flesh.

> *And the eyes of them both were opened, and they knew*
> *that they were naked; and they sewed fig leaves together,*
> *and made themselves aprons.*
> *Genesis 3:7 (KJV)*

When Adam and Eve fell, the Lord came walking in the garden in the cool of the day.

*Then the man and his wife heard the sound of the LORD
God as he was walking in the garden in the **COOL** of the
day, and they hid from the LORD God among the trees of
the garden. But the LORD God called to the man, "Where
are you?"*
Genesis 3:9 (NIV)

The word 'cool' is the Hebrew word 'ruach', which means spirit.
The Lord came walking in the garden in the spirit of the day!
Whywas that? Because, as it says in John 4:24, the Lord is
spirit!

He created a spirit called Adam and was coming to commune
with him and Eve. When He came into the garden in the spirit,
He declared,

> *Adam, Where art thou?*
> *Genesis 3:9 (KJV)*

The Omniscient God could not find Adam because Adam had
died spiritually and had become flesh. Adam had lost His
creation and became a formation, a living, earthbound and
terrestrial being.

> *So it is written: "The first man Adam became a living being";
> the last Adam, a life-giving spirit.*
> *1 Corinthians 15:45 (NIV)*

god of this world

Many people think that Lucifer gained the title, 'god of this world'. However, Lucifer was the intended god of this world from the beginning. Before the garden belonged to Adam, the Scripture is clear, it belonged to Lucifer.

> *You were in Eden, the garden of God; every precious stone adorned you: carnelian, chrysolite and emerald, topaz, onyx and jasper, lapis lazuli, turquoise and beryl. Your settings and mountings were made of gold; on the day you were created they were prepared. Ezekiel 28:13 (NIV)*

Adam and Eve were put in the Earth with the assignment to subdue it and to have dominion!

> *And God blessed them, and God said unto them, Be fruitful, and multiply, and replenish the earth, and subdue it: and have dominion over the fish of the sea, and over the fowl of the air, and over every living thing that moveth upon the earth. Genesis 1:28 (KJV)*

However, they did not dominate, but instead were dominated by one to whom the Earth and garden originally belonged. According to Ezekiel 28, earth was Lucifer's original home. We will attempt to explain this later

Be Born Again

> *Flesh gives birth to flesh, but the Spirit gives birth to spirit. You should not be surprised at my saying, 'You must be born again.'*
> *John 3:5-6 (NIV)*

Adam was put in the earth as the new designated 'god of this world. His first assignment was to subdue a snake that was thrown down to the earth hoping to get his power back.

The creation that God created to rule the cosmos on His behalf (Adam) became supplanted by one more craftily disguised and more cosmopolitan than he. The serpent forever became known as a symbol of disguise and even became a similitude of Christ defeating the enemy on the Cross by disguising Himself in flesh.

> Just as Moses lifted up the snake in the wilderness, so the Son of Man must be lifted up,
> John 3:14 (NIV)

In the Old Testament, man became flesh and was cursed to death. The last Adam, Jesus, came as a lifegiving spirit to redeem man back to the spirit realm through His death on the Cross. To be born again simply means to come back into your creation .

> Then God said, "Let us make mankind in our image, in our likeness, so that they may rule over the fish in the sea and the birds in the sky, over the livestock and all the wild animals, and over all the creatures that move along the ground."
> Genesis 1:26 (NIV)

Without your spiritual life, you are subject to the god of this world. You can gain the whole world serving the wicked god of this world, but in the process you, like Adam, will forfeit your soul.

What good will it be for someone to gain the whole world,
yet forfeit their soul? Or what can anyone give in exchange
for their soul?
Matthew 16:26 (NIV)

We are on a mission to regain the whole world, but it is not a mission that has not already been won in the spirit by Jesus Christ our Messiah and His blood on the Cross.

"I have told you these things, so that in me you may have
peace. In this world you will have trouble. But take heart! I
have overcome the world."
John 16:33 (NIV)

You and I will do greater works than Christ did, but not because we are greater than Christ, no! For He is the Name above every other Name. It is because He has gone back to the Father and has therefore left His record behind for you and I to break!

Very truly I tell you, whoever believes in me will do the
works I have been doing, and they will do even greater
things than these, because I am going to the Father.
John 14:12 (NIV)

It is because Christ has already conquered in the spirit realm that we get to invoke His name to conquer in the natural realm that which His blood has already paid for in the spiritual realm. That makes us MORE THAN CONQUERORS!

In all these things we are more than conquerors through
him who loved us.
Romans 8:37 (NIV)

Rocky Balboa is one of best loved movie heroes. His character is known for never giving up and for always getting back up when knocked down. Rocky is also known for his deep love for his wife Adrianna. Now we know that championship boxing is an individual sport. One on one. In the films, we see Rocky facing his opponent, taking the blows and landing the punches. Yet his championship victory benefitted his whole family and entourage, including in particular, for the purposes of this illustration, the champion's wife. In the film series, we see how Rocky's winning turned his fortunes from struggling to get by into lavish riches. Adrian, the champion's bride, did not have had to face the enemy in the ring or suffer any injuries. Yet, she received the spoils of the sporting battle – the rewards, the winnings and the lifestyle.

It is the same with Christ and us His bride. Christ, the husband overcame the wicked one so that we His church can share in the spoils of His victory. Christ is a conqueror, we His bride are more than conquerors.

Read on and learn how to be engaged to take your cosmopolitan position and redeem the spoils of a victory Christ died for. Rest assured all the while that you are not in the cosmopolite to finish what Jesus started but rather to start what He already finished!

Jesus said, "It is finished."
John 19:30 (NIV)

Chapter Three
Worlds Apart
The earth versus the world

We are not ignorant

We begin this chapter from the premise that Satan is now known as 'the god of this world' and master usurper who stole his authority from Adam. I also hope that by now you are comfortable with recognising that 'god' is not a name, but an office and that men and even fallen angels can equally hold this office as it speaks to rulership and judgment now praise and worship.

Having understanding of this kingdom, dubbed 'the kingdom of darkness', will help us, if we are going to infect it with the Kingdom of God. It is purely a cosmetic kingdom ruled entirely by fallen angels and unclean spirits. It is a new world order under constant rebranding by Satan.

Apostle Paul encourages the Body of Christ not to be ignorant of the devil's devices. Some in Christianity have ignored the devil to such and extent that they have convinced themselves that he does not even exist. If you are one of those, I suggest it is because Satan's kingdom is entirely cosmetic and, just like cosmetics, it has concealed blemishes and beautified its surface value in order to present a superficial representation of what is truly hiding behind it.

So that we would not be outwitted by Satan; for we are not ignorant of his schemes.2 Corinthians 2:11 (ESV)

According to the Merrian-Webster dictionary, a scheme is 'a systematic or organised configuration'. Satan is highly organised and systematic. An organised devil cannot be defeated by a disorganised church.

> If a kingdom is divided against itself, that kingdom cannot stand.
> Mark 3:24 (NIV)

Apostle Paul warns the church that if it remains ignorant, then Satan's designs and schemes will always defraud us like it did our patriarch and matriarch, Adam and Eve. The devil does not play the power game; he plays the wit game! If we are going to succeed, we have to get used to understanding that the devil's strength is his ability to defraud us of what God wants for us. Look what the Bible says about him.

> "Son of man, take up a lament concerning the king of Tyre and say to him: 'This is what the Sovereign LORD says: "'You were the seal of perfection, full of wisdom and perfect in beauty.
> Ezekiel 28:12 (NIV)

The seal of all perfection is brains and beauty, we all know that. However, by using the word 'were' it connotes that Satan has lost one or both of these somehow. Lucifer, as Satan was once known, was the complete package; superficially flawless and supernaturally smart. He used the power of beauty to beguile Adam and Eve and to defraud them of their inheritance.

*When the woman saw that the fruit of the tree was good for
food and pleasing to the eye, and also desirable for gaining
wisdom, she took some and ate it. She also gave some to
her husband, who was with her, and he ate it.*
Genesis 3:6 (NIV)

The Bible says Satan corrupted his wisdom on account of his
beauty, meaning that Satan is an extreme fascist. His beauty
destroyed him and he lost the supernatural for the superficial.
Through beauty, Satan has been tricking the church and the
inhabitants of the world ever since.

*Your heart became proud on account of your beauty, and
you corrupted your wisdom because of your splendor. So I
threw you to the earth; I made a spectacle of you before
kings.*
Ezekiel 28:17 (NIV)

Satan is no longer the perfect being, but is merely a vain
representation of what he was and so through disguising evil in
beauty, he is able to deceive the world. After all, how can
something that looks and sounds so good be so evil?

*The god of this age has blinded the minds of unbelievers,
so that they cannot see the light of the gospel that displays
the glory of Christ, who is the image of God.*
2 Corinthians 4:4 (NIV)

This battle against the devil is not a battle of power, it is a
battle of beauty or branding. The two come together to make
up what Ezekiel calls 'the seal of perfection'.

Paul says that the goal of this cosmic battle between man and the devil is for the church not to be outwitted or *pleonekteó* in the Greek.

> *pleonekteó: to have more, to overreach*
> *Original Word: πλεονεκτέω*
> *Part of Speech: Verb*
> *Transliteration: pleonekteó*
> *Phonetic Spelling: (pleh-on-cek-teh'-o)*
> *Short Definition: I take advantage of*
> *Definition: I take advantage of, overreach, defraud.*

Don't let the devil take advantage of you and, as with Adam, defraud you of what's yours by outwitting you! The word outwit means 'to get the better of by superior cleverness.' The enemy uses superior cleverness to defraud us.

It is time for us, the church to apply a far more superior intelligence than his. It is time for us to get back to the superior intelligence of the mind of Christ.

> *But he that is spiritual judgeth all things, yet he himself is judged of no man. For who hath known the mind of the Lord, that he may instruct him? But we have the mind of Christ.*
> *1 Corinthians 2:15-16 (KJV)*

Understanding Satan's Devices

Satan's biggest device is to convince the world at large that he indeed does not exist. Like any good soldier knows the best way to win a war is through stealth.

When convinced that your enemy is not you enemy, like in the instance of Eve, you can ignorantly engage in conversation and fraternise with the very snake that you are called to kill. This is what the Bible means when it says:

> Now the serpent was more *subtil* than any beast of the field which the LORD God had made. And he said unto the woman, Yea, hath God said, Ye shall not eat of every tree of the garden?
> Genesis 3:1 KJV

'Subtil' is the archaic spelling of 'subtle'. The original Hebrew word is 'arum'. A word study of 'arum' reveals some interesting points.

> *arum: crafty, shrewd, sensible*
> *Original Word: עָרוּם*
> *Part of Speech: Adjective*
> *Transliteration: arum*
> *Phonetic Spelling: (aw-room')*
> *Short Definition: man,*
> *crafty, shrewd, sensible*

Now let's begin to construct a list of Satan's devices:

Stealth and subtlety

Subtlety is the foundation block of Satan's devices. Subtle means 'elusive', 'difficult to perceive' or 'operating insidiously'. The enemy is very elusive and capable through subtlety of deceiving many people both inside and outside the church. If we are going to raise a clarion call for the cosmopolitan Christian, we have to understand that Satan constructs a world system around an ability to evade detection! We could almost use the word 'stealth' in defining him. He masterfully camouflages himself in the ornaments of life in order to convince an ever advancing intellectual and technologically savvy world of his non existence.

The logo of the World Health Organization (WHO) depicts a snake coiled around a staff, which the WHO explains is taken from Greek mythology and symbolized medicine and medical profession. Satan has rebranded himself as a helpful serpent! Mythologies and religions of the world all have the same serpent at their root. This is Satan shrouding himself in myth so that his motives can evade detection.

I am originally from Africa, Nigeria to be more specific. My relatives would laugh at me and often mock me as being a Westerner, seeing as I only lived in Nigeria till I was two years old and have spent virtually all of my life in the United Kingdom. My Christian relatives would say things like:

> *"Tomi, you in the West don't understand real demons. If you want to know about real demons, come to Africa! That's where all the demonic activity happens."*

They used to tell me stories that were quite honestly hard for my Western-thinking mind to believe. Stories of how demons could manifest and beat them up as little imps, or how a woman they knew used to turn into a snake at night. Stories that quite literally beggared belief, but were shared so prolifically and with such consensus from others across the nation that it made one feel quite stupid for not believing it!

I do believe that there is a type of raw faith in outside of the West that we must hunger for. It is this faith that releases godly activity all over Africa. Likewise, miracles are often an anomaly here in the West, but are a frequent occasion of the Eastern world.

The Lord shared something with me that forever changed my paradigm on the demonic and the devil's devices. Below is a paraphrase from a segment of that dialogue.

> *"Son, it is not the devil you see that is the most sophisticated, it is the devil you don't!"*

Whilst the third world has a first world God, we in the Western world have a first world devil! If you can see the devil, then his device is primitive. If you can see the witch doctor and the warts on the witch's nose, then you are dealing with a primitive device of the enemy. It is a device that many in the West have relegated to children's books and fantasy movies. The greatest device of the enemy is to instill himself within intellectual systems and organisations without us even knowing he is there.

In the West, we have industrialised and caricatured the demonic so that even the suggestion of a manifestation being anything other than a mental illness is deemed politically incorrect and, in some instances, is considered to be 'hate speech' that could land a church in serious legal jeopardy. The enemy has hedged himself well and therefore we have a more sophisticated demonic network in the West than in the East where victory over the enemy is evidenced by his coming out of hiding!

The sensible thing

'Arum' also means sensible. Another of Satan's stealth tactics is to be very sensible! To the reasoned person, he makes a lot of sense! This ability to switch between pragmatism and idealism has worked masterfully to his advantage. He will tell Jesus 'why suffer and die for the world when you can have it and all and all you have to do is bend a knee' (See Matthew 4:9). He tells David, why pray when you can count resources and see if you have enough to do what you used to accomplish by trusting in God (See 1 Chronicles 21 and 2 Samuel 24).

His rationale and ability to reason with us is a skill that gets us to momentarily pacify obedience and temporarily suspend our own convictions, which after the fact, leaves us in shame, wondering what on earth came over us.

> For the good that I would I do not: but the evil which I would not, that I do. Now if I do that I would not, it is no more I that do it, but sin that dwelleth in me.
> Romans 7:19-20 (KJV)

Good intentions

God **IS** good. Satan **DOES** good!

The principal foundation of the Christian life is and ought to be that God is good! However, what we also need to recognize, if we are going to be the army of God in a cosmopolitan world, is that Satan does good!

45

How? It's all about presentation!

Satan dresses up lies in truths and bad in good intentions to the point that any dissent is considered a public enemy of good and, ultimately, an adversary of progress. When you think about the tree from which he tempted Adam and Eve to eat, it is the very summation of his master strategy.

> But from the tree of the knowledge of **GOOD AND EVIL** you shall not eat, for in the day that you eat from it you shall surely die."
> Genesis 2:17 (NASBS)

Satan's second most effective device in the framework of the cosmos is using good intentions to do as much evil as possible!

Good is the cosmetic make-up that he uses to conceal evil. This is how so many, including the church, get sucked in.

Concealing evil within a good cause

When the thought of abortion comes into a Christian's mind, we think of the murder of innocent lives, aka infanticide. When put into a cosmopolitan filter, abortion as defined by the United Kingdom National Health service as:

> "...the medical process of ending a pregnancy so it doesn't result in the birth of a baby." – NHS

When asked why, the answer is simple. Freedom of choice! The rights a woman has over her body.

In America today, infanticide is carried out under the taxpayer funded guise of 'Family Planning.' If you dare argue for the rights of the child to exist, then you would be considered to be simply lacking sufficient reason and modernity to appreciate the rights of a woman to choose. Furthermore, would be accused of failing to understand that if a woman has been raped or has a child as a product of incest then by your detrimental argument, you are forcing that woman to have a rapist's child! The enemy is succeeding in the promotion of an evil act because of a 'good' cause and on the basis of an argument that well … makes sense! A cause that only makes up just on average 1% of all abortion cases has become the truth statement upon and through which more than a billion lives have been wasted before they could draw their first breath.

Furthermore, when we take the make-up off of abortion, what we are suggesting is that the solution to a woman who has been violated is to violate her further by making her take a dangerous pill or endure an extremely evasive procedure in which the baby is ripped out piece by piece from the womb and then reassembled on the table before being disposed of.

The enemy has rebranded death to make something unacceptable, acceptable. He has done this by switching the meaning of death. You would think that the opposite of 'pro-life' would be 'pro-death'. Through Satan's cunning deceit he has beautified death by rebranding it under the guise of 'pro-choice'. This sleight of hand has led the church and conservative mind into an arena that we simply cannot win at unless we regain the battle for the etymology of words and meaning of words.

Another example of this would be the term 'conservative' versus the term 'liberal'. The Christian worldview has been branded as conservative, yet the un-Christian worldview has been branded as liberal. The church are the liberals and it is our prerogative in Christ to liberate the world from the bondage of sin that leads to death. Jesus warns us however not to use our freedom as an occasion to the flesh.

Today, through rebranding, we are now the conservative which comes with connotations that we are somehow here to drive the world backwards. When we lose the etymological argument, we give ground to the enemy to redefine the meaning of words and indeed worse, make them up out of thin air.

Words like euthanasia meaning 'good death' is another form of rebranding the enemy uses to justify culling the elderly. A practice that is already legal in some countries including the Netherlands and Canada. Again, you can apply this principle to LGBTQ rights, gay marriage and other so called 'progressive' issues which have managed to attach themselves symbiotically to the civil rights movements of African Americans and you will find that the success of these campaigns have always been on the basis of doing as much evil as possible in the guise of as much cosmetic 'good' as possible.

When the enemy doesn't like the answer, he simply changes the question to suit the answer. If gender is the problem, then let's redefine gender. An attack on the meaning of words is an attack on Jesus who is called the word (See John 1).

Woe to those who call evil good and good evil, who
substitute darkness for light and light for darkness, who
substitute bitter for sweet and sweet for bitter.
Isaiah 5:20 (NASBS)

Disguise

Clothing, it's all about clothing!

When you understand that the whole Bible is simply about clothing then you will not fail as this new breed of cosmopolitan Christian.

Ask yourself this: What did Adam and Eve lose in the garden? You may say authority, godliness, their spiritual life and all those things are true. However, more specifically and to the point, Adam and Eve lost their clothes.

The Bible demonstrates this in calling them naked in Genesis 2:25 and then naked again in Genesis 3:10. You simply cannot be naked twice!

Adam and his wife were both naked, and they felt no
shame.
Genesis 2:25 NIV

He answered, "I heard you in the garden, and I was afraid
because I was naked; so I hid."
Genesis 3:10 NIV

This tells us something interesting! Adam and Eve's bodies were hidden in the clothing of their spiritual life! When they lost their spiritual life and their physical (formed) eyes opened, they beheld a nakedness and shame that they were not accustomed to. They lost the supernatural and became superficial.

Satan usurped their clothes! It's interesting when you look at Potiphar's wife, a woman who tried to seduce righteous Joseph. She pressed him every day and tempted him, but the one thing she wanted more than his virginity was his clothes.

> And she caught him by his garment, saying, Lie with me: and he left his garment in her hand, and fled, and got him out.
> Genesis 39:12 (NIV)

Satan wants clothes! The idea that he can disguise himself in light paralleled with his message of so-called 'goodness' makes shooting the messenger virtually impossible.

> And no wonder, for even Satan disguises himself as an angel of light.
> 2 Corinthians 11:14 (ESV)

The enemy loves to play dress up and his success is his ability to masterfully reinvent himself in another arena once he has been found out. He is totally vein and entirely cosmetic and his causes are fully superficial.

It is these three 1. subtlety, 2. 'good' and 3. disguise that make the enemy a winner in the world arena. A cosmetic colosseum that God has put you, his greatest gladiators in and has surrounded you with a cloud of witnesses chanting in unison your name. God has invested His very essence inside you (The Holy Spirit) so that you and I can turn the cosmopolitan world into the Kingdom of God.

*The seventh angel sounded his trumpet, and there were
loud voices in heaven, which said: "The kingdom of the
world has become the kingdom of our Lord and of his
Messiah, and he will reign for ever and ever."
Revelation 11:15*

Earth versus World - The Difference?!?

We have already established that initially our job was to rule
the cosmos. Adam being the second 'god of this world' and its
original custodian, lost his authority to Satan the original
custodian who is once again called 'god of this world'.

*In whose case the god of this world has blinded the minds
of the unbelieving so that they might not see the light of the
gospel of the glory of Christ, who is the image of God.
2 Corinthians 4:4 (NASBS)*

Because we are no longer born solely of this world, but are
born again in Christ, we now have legal right to overcome the
world.

*For everyone born of God overcomes the world. This is the
victory that has overcome the world, even our faith.
1 John 5:4 (NIV)*

Our assignment is simple. Go into the world (cosmetics) and
turn the lights on! Let people see darkness for what it is and
decide whether they prefer it or want light.

*For you were once darkness, but now you are light in the
Lord. Live as children of light (for the fruit of the light*

*consists in all goodness, righteousness and truth) and find
out what pleases the Lord. Have nothing to do with the
fruitless deeds of darkness, but rather expose them. It is
shameful even to mention what the disobedient do in
secret. But everything exposed by the light becomes visible
—and everything that is illuminated becomes a light.
Ephesians 5:8-13 (NIV)*

However, first you need to understand fully the arena you are
going into! It is an arena that will not just expose its soft under
belly and say here is where you sink the blade in. No, you are
going to need to know the terrain well, how it operates- it
belongs to a usurper who is literally hell bent on you not
getting in.

The Earth is the Lord's, but the world is the devil's!

The world and the Earth are two different things! Think of the
Earth for a second like a field. Imagine, if you will, that the field
has a house on it that was built by a tenant who leased your
land. Anybody who claimed rights on the house would be
called a tenant. They would have a legal right to use the house
for as long as the lease lasts. But the land and all that is in it
belongs to the landlord! When the lease agreement expires,
the leaseholder has got to move out of the land and decide
whether they want to take anything like furniture, lamps or
other chattels with them. They can take the furniture but they
cannot take the house! The property now belongs to the land
lord because it was built on his land.

The earth is the Lord's freehold estate, the world is the
leasehold that the enemy has built on the freehold estate

called Earth. Eventually, his leasehold will run out. We know this because the Bible tells us this.

> *Therefore, rejoice, O heavens and you who dwell in them!*
> *But woe to you, O earth and sea, for the devil has come*
> *down to you in great wrath, because he knows that his time*
> *is short!"*
> *Revelation 12:12 (ESV)*

Soon, Satan will have to vacate the premise and give the land and the world back to the owner of the freehold. for he knows his time is short. The covenant of land belongs to those for whom the blood of Jesus was shed. All land is a blood covenant and once Jesus spilt his on the land redeeming it, then everything on it belonged to Him.

> *For, "The earth is the Lord's, and* everything *in it."*
> *1 Corinthians 10:26 (NIV)*

In the parable of the Kingdom of Heaven, Jesus illustrates this principle saying.

> *"The kingdom of heaven is like treasure hidden in a field.*
> *When a man found it, he hid it again, and then in his joy*
> *went and sold all he had and bought that field.*
> *Matthew 13:44*

The blood of Jesus did not purchase the treasure (in this case the world of which you and I consist) the blood of Jesus purchased the field of which you and I consist. In purchasing the field (in this case the earth) Jesus owns the treasure.

When righteous people understand the founding principle that owning the Earth means that you own the world, we will understand what Christ meant by this statement:

> "I have told you these things, so that in me you may have peace. In this world you will have trouble. But take heart! I have overcome the world."
> John 16:33 (NIV)

The word 'overcome' in the Greek is *nikaó*. It means to conquer or subdue. The very instruction that God gave Adam in Genesis 1:26-27 is fulfilled by Christ later on the Cross. Only one question remains unanswered: how can we Christians have 'TROUBLE' in a world that Jesus claims He has already overcome? If you are the conqueror of the world, why then don't your people have world peace?

I can imagine that when Satan tempted Jesus, he showed him the cosmetic or cosmopolitan world in the twinkling of an eye (Matthew 4:8) and he told Him:

> "All this I will give you," he said, "if you will bow down and worship me."
> Matthew 4:9 (NIV)

I would imagine that it would have seemed, in Jesus' mind, an impassioned reason to settle as He knew the suffering that awaited Him on the Cross. However, he also knew that as sensible as Satan's offer was, that Satan was capable of convincing people to sell their car to pay for their petrol. Jesus probably thought in His mind that the world may well be

Satan's, but the Earth upon which he built this world belongs to Me and I will not sell it for the 'world!' (Literally).

When Jesus declared that He had conquered, might it be that He was talking about conquering the Earth that the world was situated on. Let's explore this argument and find out!

Adam and the Adamah

Jesus did not come to redeem the world, He came to redeem the Earth and in doing so He purchased everything in it, including the world!

> 'Now then, if you will indeed obey My voice and keep My covenant, then you shall be My own possession among all the peoples, for all the earth is Mine;
> Exodus 19:5 (NASBS)

The Earth is the Lord's, otherwise Jesus would have needed Satan's permission to enter it! God creates an Earth in Genesis and then He forms a world for Adam to live in. Part of that world was included a garden in Eden. When Adam lost that world, Satan conformed a world where the only way for man to succeed was to join that counterfeit world.

Have you ever heard the saying, 'we are worlds apart'? Literally, the Lord's plan and Satan's plan are worlds apart.

An earth is real estate, a world is an intellectual property built on top of that real estate, even using the materials of that real estate.

> Then God said, "Let us make mankind in our image, in our likeness, so that they may rule over the fish in the sea and

the birds in the sky, over the livestock and all the wild
animals, and over all the creatures that move along the
ground."
Genesis 1:26 (NIV)

God was very explicit as to that over which He gave man
rulership. A rulership that now belongs to the devil. God did not
give man the sea, He gave man the fish in the sea!

Which is why only Jesus was capable of commanding it!
Causing Peter to say:

"What **KIND** *of man is this? Even the winds and the waves*
obey him!"
Matthew 8:27 (NIV)

You see, Jesus was of the 'God Kind' of man. God did not give
man the air; He said to rule over the birds of the air! God gave
man leasehold authority over the ecology and cosmology of
the Earth, not the Earth itself. That means fish in the sea, birds
in the air and over every creeping thing that moves on the
ground.

The word land is the Hebrew word *'Adamah'*. It means soil. It is
from where we get the name Adam or 'man of soil'. Adam in
the Hebrew means 'bloody man' or to 'show blood'. So, blood
is the only thing uniting the Adam with the blessing of the
Adamah. One might say that Adam and the Earth had a blood
covenant! Life is in the blood!

Because the life of every creature is its blood.
Leviticus 17:14 (NIV)

The blood determines life not the soil! Because our blood was eternal before the Fall, our life was eternal. When man sinned, our blood was no longer pure and became capable of disease, fault and blemish, but in the beginning man was alive because he had blood flowing through him. The essential quality of all life is blood! The ground or Adamah recognised Adam's authority because of the blood that flowed through him. A bloodline, that traces his lineage to God Himself. It was this bloodline that made it impossible for the Earth to not respond to Adam like it responded to God. Adam didn't need to even speak to the ground to obey Him, His blood spoke for Him!

and to Jesus, the mediator of a new covenant, and to the
sprinkled blood that speaks…
Hebrews 12:24 (NIV)

Imagine a world that responds to you because of your blood. Isn't that the world of royal families? How much more the royal family of the Kingdom of God! When Adam sinned, God spoke three principle curses to three principle characters that were a part of that fall.

Character 1 - The Serpent (a curse)
Character 2- The Woman (a consequence)
Character 3- The ground (a curse)

Notice God cursed the serpent with a slithering, handless and footless life. He told the woman that she was going to bring forth children painfully. Why? Because up until that time, people were only born in the spirit, but now that Adam and Eve were flesh they would have to give birth in a way that was not the way God initially intended. This is why childbearing painfully was not a curse, but was a consequence of the flesh life. And then to Adam, God said this:

> *"...cursed is the Adamah (ground) because of you!"*
> *Genesis 3:17 (NIV)*

What is so interesting about this is that God did not curse Adam! He did not even curse the ground! He declared that the ground was cursed as a consequence of Adam eating something that he was not supposed to eat. If the Adamah is cursed then the Adam is cursed. It's almost like God is saying that Adam ate death and the Adamah got an upset stomach! God then goes on to list what the curse entailed. (Genesis 3:17)

1. *The earth will produce both pretty flowers and terribly evil things (thorns and thistles)*
2. *Before you were just there to tend and keep but, now you'll have to learn to sow and reap!*
3. *You will live in your formation (the dust) and because you are no longer spirit, the ground or Adamah itself will redeem you and generations after you as an endless, payless ransom for your trespass!*

This is what the Earth did as a response to Adam. A ground that once obeyed his royal blood refused to respond to him without intense work, effort and labour called a seed! The same applied to everything that came from the Adamah, including Eve.

The first time the Earth tasted impure blood, it did not like the taste! In fact, the Bible says when Cain slew his brother Abel that the ground itself cursed Abel!

> And now you are cursed from the ground (Adamah), which has opened its mouth to receive your brother's blood from your hand.
> Genesis 4:11 (NASBS)

When people died in the Old Testament, their bodies returned to the ground. Until Jesus, there had not been a blood (seed) pure enough to break the curse of death that sin had brought about and to return the Earth back to the Kingdom of the Adams. Until Christ, innocent lambs were only a temporary solution to a groaning earth that was longing to be liberated from its curse.

The average adult body contains only 5.5 litres of blood. How can 5.5 litres of blood possibly cover the sins of the every human being upon the earth. Jesus did not need to spill his blood on fallen Adam, He just needed to spill His blood on fallen Adamah. Once His blood spilt on the Earth it broke the curse of sin and death as His sacrifice eternally redeemed man from the curse of sin and death.

> And being in anguish, he prayed more earnestly, and his sweat was like drops of blood falling to the ground.
> Luke 22:44 (NIV)

When the ground received his blood, it was like the time it received the blood of Abel but this blood spoke better things and a better and newer covenant!

*To Jesus the mediator of a new covenant, and to the
sprinkled blood that speaks a better word than the blood of
Abel.*
Hebrews 12:24 (NIV)

When Jesus redeemed the Adamah, he redeemed 'the
Adams'. Through the blood shed on the earth 2000 years ago,
Earth is now fully satisfied that a pure ransom has been paid
and the grave is no longer the end of man! It is this, that Christ
meant when He said that He had overcome the world!

*And through him to reconcile to himself all things, whether
things on earth or things in heaven, by making peace
through his blood, shed on the cross.*
Colossians 1:20 (NIV)

Jesus redeemed the Adamah and with it Adam (mankind), and
by His blood a New Covenant doesn't mean that we won't all
die and go to the dust, but that we who believe in Christ will
live on past death. For Christ did not come to abolish the law
(death) He came to fulfil it by Himself dying but then rising
again! (Matthew 5:17)

There are three parts to the demise of Satan.
- Part 1 - God overcame Him by throwing Him out of
  heaven to Earth! (Revelation 12:7)
- Part 2 - Jesus overcame Him in His victory on the
  Cross (Colossians 2:15)
- Part 3 is still being written. It is when we, the church,
  apply that victory of the Cross that has redeemed the
  ground from the curse and go into the world and

overcome him, the devil, by the victory of Christ's Blood and His Word!

And they overcame him by the blood of the Lamb, and by the word of their testimony; and they loved not their lives unto the death. Revelation 12:11 (KJV)

This will be an ushering in of the greatest move of God's Spirit the earth has ever known. Believers who understand the victory of the Cross will move into world systems operating from a higher Kingdom and will restore all intellectual property back to its Landlord, Jesus Christ!

This is why Christ is called a conqueror. He conquered death and the Earth's curse and as a result, we, His church, get to be more than a conqueror (Romans 8:37) as we go into the cosmos and bring it back under Jesus' authority. This is when the final trumpet will sound and we will all hear God say well done good and faithful servant.

The seventh angel sounded his trumpet, and there were loud voices in heaven, which said: "The kingdom of the world has become the kingdom of our Lord and of his Messiah, and he will reign for ever and ever." Revelation 11:15 (NIV)

However, until then, we have work to do. We are not here to finish what Christ started, we are here to start what He has already finished. Jesus has finished, He's waiting for us to start so He can return.

"'The Lord said to my Lord: "Sit at my right hand until I put your enemies under your feet."'
Matthew 22:44 (NIV)

We are here to put Christ's enemies under Christ's feet.

Chapter Four

A Cosmetic Kingdom
Taking back Intellectual Property

We have established that Satan's world is different from God's earth. The Earth is the Lord's and the world is the devil's. We also know that we as 'cosmopolitan Christians' have an assignment to reclaim Satan's world and turn it back to the Lord's world, *on earth as it is in heaven!*

We also understand from scripture that Satan is called the god of this world (2 Corinthians 4:4) and that his assignment is to blind eyes from seeing the glorious Gospel of Jesus Christ who is the image of God! Now let's look at the materials that define the cosmological world and its arrangement under Satan's design.

> *In whom the god of this world hath blinded the minds of them which believe not, lest the light of the glorious gospel of Christ, who is the image of God, should shine unto them.*
> *2 Corinthians 4:4 (KJV)*

A Cosmetic World

> *"The kingdom of the world has become the kingdom of our Lord and of his Messiah, and he will reign for ever and ever."*
> *Revelation 11:15 (NIV)*

The word in Revelation 11:15 for 'world' in the Greek is *'kosmos'*. According to Strong's concordance, it means:

World
Worldly affairs
World systems
World order

From *'kosmos'* we get *'kosmētikós'* from which comes the word 'cosmetic', meaning:

1. to adorn
2. to fashion
3. to put make up on
4. To furnish
5. To decorate

The world is the decoration of the Earth!

The world is the intellectual property that fashions the earth. It is dictated by the devil! (the god of this world). He has patented it, so that the only way to get in on his trademark is to literally sell him your soul.

> *What good is it for someone to gain the whole world, yet forfeit their soul?*
> *Mark 8:36 (NIV)*

Satan's ambition is to create a world where people are blinded from the image of Christ and so he will put systems in place and world orders in place that will help him to achieve that end.

I want to draw your attention back to the Book of Matthew, chapter 4, when Jesus was being tried by the devil.

The tempter came to him and said, "If you are the Son of God, tell these stones to become bread." Jesus answered, "It is written: 'Man shall not live on bread alone, but on every word that comes from the mouth of God.'"

Then the devil took him to the holy city and had him stand on the highest point of the temple. "If you are the Son of God," he said, "throw yourself down. For it is written: " 'He will command his angels concerning you, and they will lift you up in their hands, so that you will not strike your foot against a stone.' " Jesus answered him, "It is also written: 'Do not put the Lord your God to the test.' "

Again, the devil took him to a very high mountain and showed him all the kingdoms of the world and their splendor. "All this I will give you," he said, "if you will bow down and worship me." Jesus said to him, "Away from me, Satan! For it is written: 'Worship the Lord your God, and serve him only.' "
Matthew 4:3-10 (NIV)

There were three principle things that Satan tried Jesus on:

1. *Lust of the flesh*
2. *Lust of the eyes*
3. *The pride of life*

These have been the three temptations that are always going to be a part of this world order and its trappings.

For everything in the world--the lust of the flesh, the lust of
the eyes, and the pride of life--comes not from the Father
but from the world.
1 John 2:16 (NIV)

Jesus was asked by the devil to turn stones into bread. His response was that it is written that man shall not live on bread alone, but on every word that comes from the mouth of God.

He was then taken to the Holy City! Yes, you heard it, Satan took Jesus to church!

Then the devil took him to the holy city and had him stand
on the highest point of the temple. "If you are the Son of
God," he said, "throw yourself down. For it is written: 'He
will command his angels concerning you,
and they will lift you up in their hands, so that you will not
strike your foot against a stone.'
Matthew 4:5 (NIV)

Satan took Jesus to the Holy City and then to the Holy Temple. Notice, Satan is not moved by the holiness of the place despite even the priests not taking their common people into for the fear of the Lord.

Finally, Satan took Jesus up to a high mountain and showed Him all the kingdoms of the world (cosmos) and their glory!

Why is this important?

Well, let's call Satan's kingdom what it is, a cosmetic kingdom! It is nothing more than an aesthetically pleasing prop made to blind people from God!

However, within this cosmetic kingdom also exists cosmetic churches! Churches or sanctuaries are considered holy places. The Bible says that where Holiness is, the devil cannot be.

> *And a highway will be there;*
> *it will be called the Way of Holiness;*
> *it will be for those who walk on that Way.*
> *The unclean will not journey on it;*
> *wicked fools will not go about on it.*
> *No lion will be there,*
> *nor any ravenous beast;*
> *they will not be found there.*
> *But only the redeemed will walk there,*
> *Isaiah 35:8-9 (NIV)*
>
> *… your adversary, the devil, as a roaring lion, walketh about, seeking whom he may devour.*
> *1 Peter 5:8 (KJV)*

How is it possible, if no lion can put their foot on the highway of holiness, that he who is 'like a roaring lion' (Satan) can take Jesus to a Holy City and a Holy Temple? Is it possible that many of our churches have become part of the props? I call these churches 'cosmetic churches'!

The Cosmetic Church

How do you know if you go to a cosmetic church? A church that is part of the cosmos that is owned by the enemy and is a place, like the temple, where he is not afraid to tread.

You must make up your mind that you are not going to commit yourself to a cosmetic church if you are ever going to be the cosmopolitan change-agent!

Below is a grid, intended to help you decipher the difference between a living church and a cosmetic one.

LIVING CHURCH	COSMETIC CHURCH
Sensitive seekers	seeker sensitive
One BODY many Parts	Many BODIES one Part
Growing	Cloning
Prays	Plays
Strength in Oneness	Strength in Numbers
Power	No Power
Sending	Controlling
Grows	Gathers
Righteous	Religious
Truth Defending	Defending against Truth
Faith Based	Fear Based
Vision	Ambition
Spirit Led	Man Driven
Signs & Wonders	Staged & Wonderful

Confrontational	Congregational
Prophetic	Popular
Revelatory	Revolving
Governmental	Theological
Seasonal	Sermonal
Igniting	Exciting
Transformational	Motivational
Evangelical	Empirical
Spirit led	Schedule led
Apostolic/Prophetic led	Pastoral/Teacher led
Does what God is blessing	Asks God to bless what they're doing
City Changers	City unaffected
Saints equipped	Saints enabled
Kingdom culture	Democratic culture
Spiritual	Social

We live in a cosmetic world and it is important for the purposes of gathering that our churches have branding, slogans, jingles and serve teas and coffees. However, if all of that is a replacement for the power and presence of God, or the lack thereof, then it is nothing more than a cosmetic church in a cosmetic world.

Satan is not afraid of our worship as long as our worship is cosmetic! He doesn't fear cosmetic holiness, cosmetic prayer, cosmetic relationships, cosmetic pastors, cosmetic charisma, cosmetic preaching, cosmetic tears or cosmetic buildings! The only thing Satan fears is a living church, demonstrating the power, not substituting it for face value or seeker sensitive bells and whistles.

A well-known preacher, Apostle Ryan Le Strange, says,

> *"If you have to outsource the majority of your spiritual growth from someone else's ministry, the chances are that you are in a dead church."*

Jesus was a cosmetic charismatic

Jesus was a cosmetic charismatic! God came to Earth disguised as man! It was this that baffled Satan's sensibilities and still astounds many in religions, like the Muslim faith, to date.

> *"Sacrifice and offering you did not desire, but a body you prepared for me"*
> *Hebrews 10:5 (NIV)*

Jesus was willing to wear the body of fallen man so that He could disguise the master plan of God in a vessel made of clay!

> *He was in the world, and though the world was made through him, the world did not recognise him.*
> *John 1:10 (NIV)*

71

Jesus wants his world back and He has a master plan that involves you and I, a new breed of cosmopolitan Christians!

There was something we can see in Scripture about Jesus and disguises. Might it be that just as Satan disguised himself as a serpent that God disguised Himself as a man so that He could take back what the devil had stolen?

> *Just as Moses lifted up the snake in the wilderness, so the*
> *Son of Man must be lifted up,*
> *John 3:14 (NIV)*

To me, that's like saying, 'you snaked me, I'm going to snake you back.'

Prophetic set ups

Jesus came into the Earth through his mother Mary, but the Bible says when He was about to enter the world (cosmos) that he prayed and he fasted for forty days. Why? Immediately beforehand he had heard the voice of God announcing who He was.

> *And a voice from heaven said, "This is my Son, whom I*
> *love; with him I am well pleased."*
> *Matthew 3:17 (NIV)*

Notice, immediately after this prophecy from John the Baptist, Jesus was led into the wilderness to be tried by the devil whose first question was:

"If you are the son of God..."
John 4:3 (NIV)

What if your predicament was set up by your last prophecy? What if revelation; as good as it makes us feel, is a set up for tribulation? What if you are struggling financially because somebody prophesied that you were going to be a successful entrepreneur? Or you are in bad health because somebody prophesied that you were going to heal the sick? I am not in any way saying God brings your trouble, but what if your revelation does exactly that - reveals you and exposes you to the flip side of the coin?

Satan did not challenge Jesus on anything else but His last prophetic word! What if your trial doesn't come to challenge who you think you are, but who God says you are? What if we are misappropriating the purpose of prophecy in our lives and although it edifies, exhorts and comforts us (1 Corinthians 14:3) ultimately, we are supposed to weaponise our prophetic words and prepare ourselves for the battle it brings.

> *Timothy, my son, I am giving you this command in keeping*
> *with the prophecies once made about you, so that by*
> *recalling them you may fight the battle well*
> *1 Timothy 1:18*

The evolution of Satan's world

Satan's focus has been singular from the beginning of time and that is to create a world that fully worships him and to translate himself in such a way that he becomes inconspicuously integrated into our cultural norms, even if that means drastically altering the definition of 'norm' itself in order to do so.

Satan's world has gone through many rebrands over time. These rebrands are part of what makes mankind so forgetful about the mistakes of history and, thus, more likely to repeat them.

There have been hurdles along the way to fulfilling Satan's strategy. One of course has been God, who along the way has declared prophecies that always seem to disrupt the flow of Satan's timing and cause him to build elsewhere. Here is a key prophecy and one that has limited Satan's capacity to fulfil his plan until now.

> *I will make your descendants as numerous as the stars in the sky and will give them all these lands, and through your offspring all nations on earth will be blessed,*
> *Genesis 26:4 (NIV)*

The plan has also been disrupted by men and women throughout history who have prayed, fasted and were willing to be cosmopolitan in order to change and hinder his plan.

Satan is finite!
He is not everywhere! He does not know everything! In fact, in the book of Job when God asks him where he has been, his response was,

> *"From going to and fro on the earth, and from walking up and down on it."*
> *Job 1:7*

This means that he, unlike the omnipotent, omnipresent and all knowing God is somewhat limited!

It is still not known exactly how many people are on earth today. It has been estimated that there are around 7.6 billion people, but there is no real way to keep a tab on them all. The Bible goes a step further to say that mankind is going to grow so much in number that they will not be able to be counted! Imagine being the 'god of this world' and not being able to know how many people are in your world!

Remember, the cosmos world may belong to Satan, but we certainly do not! We, the Bride of Christ are bought with a price in the greatest love story ever told.

> *They are not of the world, even as I am not of it.*
> *John 17:16*

The stars
Satan had a plan that in order to keep tabs on the amount of people in his intellectual property, he would need to learn to start counting stars!

> *You are wearied with your many counsels; let them stand*
> *forth and save you, those who divide the heavens, who*
> *gaze at the stars, who at the new moons make known what*
> *shall come upon you.*
> *Isaiah 47:13*

Star Signs I Are they wrong?

Whilst credit has to be given to the accuracy of such things as astrology and star gazing, it is inherently wrong to seek the stars for counsel! Why? Because God commands us against it!

> You shall not eat any flesh with the blood in it. You shall not interpret omens or tell fortunes.
> Leviticus 19:26

The enemy knows that God said that mankind will be as the stars! So within his arsenal of espionage is an ability to predict the lives and even locations of mankind through observing their star!

> And he brought him forth outside, and said, Look now toward heaven, and count the stars, if you be able to number them: and he said unto him, So shall your descendants be.
> Genesis 15:5

Even Jesus had a star 'sign!'

Jesus Himself had a star! It was this star that a group of wise men were able to use to locate the approximate whereabouts of Jesus Christ! The Bible calls these wise men, Magi.

> After Jesus was born in Bethlehem in Judea, during the time of King Herod, Magi from the east came to Jerusalem and asked, "Where is the one who has been born king of the Jews? We saw his star when it rose and have come to worship him."
> Matthew 2:1-2

These were not your average kings as many of our Sunday school teachers would have had us think. On the contrary, the word 'magi' comes from the word we now know as 'magician'., It means that wise magicians from the east came to Jerusalem. These were sorcerers who came to meet the one who was to be born King of the Jews. The word 'magi' seems to infer that these men were of oriental origin and had used their ability to read star signs to pinpoint an approximate location of where Christ would be born. Herod then utilised their gift (which again the Bible forbids us to do) to try to kill Jesus before He could be born.

> *Then Herod called the Magi secretly and found out from*
> *them the exact time the star had appeared.*
> *Matthew 2:7 NIV*

Stars signs are very real and they serve as a sign of man! Each star born represents a soul in the Earth, Satan knows this and mankind like these 'magi' utilise it, many times unbeknownst that they are practicing something demonic that is against God's will! We know them today as 'star signs' because that is what God originally called them and intended for their purpose to be.

> *And God said, "Let there be lights in the vault of the sky to*
> *separate the day from the night, and let them serve as*
> *signs to mark sacred times, and days and years,*
> *Genesis 1:14*

Stars serve as signs, but we are forbidden from practicing the reading and observing of them!

Idolatry, sorcery, enmity, strife, jealousy, fits of anger, rivalries, dissensions, divisions, envy, drunkenness, orgies, and things like these. I warn you, as I warned you before, that those who do such things will not inherit the kingdom of God.
Galatians 5:20-21

Satan wants to count

The devil is very invested in counting mankind! Why? Because anyone you can count you can control! God intended man to be innumerable because when you create a governmental system that starts counting its citizens then that system becomes controllable.

But you have said, 'I will surely make you prosper and will make your descendants like the sand of the sea, which cannot be counted.'''
Genesis 32:12

Notice, anytime a leader in the Bible wanted to control an outcome he or she first started by taking a census (people count)

In those days Caesar Augustus issued a decree that a census should be taken of the entire Roman world. (This was the first census that took place while Quirinius was governor of Syria.) And everyone went to their own town to register.
Luke 2:1-2 (NIV)

Counting is a form of controlling as God said that His descendants could be counted! It was for this very reason that God was angry with David!

> *Satan stood up against Israel and incited David to count the people of Israel.*
> *1 Chronicles 21:1 (NRSV)*

God was angry with what David had done. Notice that David was incited by Satan to do this. Satan knows that if he can count man then, ultimately, he will be able to control man! His ultimate plan will be fulfilled when he knows the exact location, time, address and number of every human being upon the face of the Earth.

Evolution 1 | Babylonian model

Babel was the first cosmopolitan, intellectual estate that Satan tried to build on God's earth using mankind. He took advantage of certain exploitable and viable characteristics written about in Genesis 11 in order to fulfil his conquest. Such as:

1. *The whole Earth was of the same language*
2. *The whole earth was of the same culture and political belief*

> *Now the whole world had one language and a common speech.*
> *Genesis 11:1*

This uniformity allowed him to incite a man called Nimrod, meaning rebellion; to build a polity, or society, that could exclude God as their ruler and make humanism the driving force of this new world order.

> *Then they said, "Come, let us build ourselves a city, with a tower that reaches to the heavens, so that we may make a name for ourselves; otherwise we will be scattered over the face of the whole earth."*
> *Genesis 11:4 (NIV)*

These people didn't want to be scattered and, I can imagine, neither did the devil. By creating a world system where everyone was all in one place and of the same political opinion and language, they were more easily controllable or governable. This truly was so much more than anything the United Nations or the United States of America could ever achieve - this was simply put a 'United Nation', where unity was not based on diversity, but on sameness!

Like David, they were incited and, unbeknownst to them, Satan was inspiring this form of government. It seemed like the perfect idea and very sensible! I can think of a million reasons to build Babel:

1. *No class systems*

2. *Dramatic decrease in unemployment*

3. *Citizens needs provided for*

4. *Strong and safe country*

5. *No discrimination*

6. *Benevolent dictators*

7. *One media source of information and communication*

Why would God come down and confuse the language of these people? Surely, these are all the things God would stand for? Remember, we said, the enemy is very sensible. We call this sensibleness- the wisdom of the world.

> *For the wisdom of this world is foolishness in God's sight.*
> *As it is written: "He catches the wise in their craftiness";*
> *1 Corinthians 3:19*

The wisdom of the world is foolishness to God! There is a crafty design behind all the 'good' of Satan's props, or as the old saying goes, 'the road to hell is paved with good intentions'. Satan's assignment is to do as much evil as possible through doing as much apparent good! Because he knows that the greatest enemy of the right thing to do is a 'good' thing to do.

> *But the Lord came down to see the city and the tower the*
> *people were building. The Lord said, "If as one people*
> *speaking the same language they have begun to do this,*
> *then nothing they plan to do will be impossible for*
> *them.Come, let us go down and confuse their language so*
> *they will not understand each other."*
> *Genesis 11:5-7 (NIV)*

The Lord broke up their plan because He knew that their imaginations were devoid of God. Any institution, constitution or organisation made on earth that is not made in heaven, God will not bless No matter how well intentioned they are, their downfall is inevitable!

Except the Lord build the house, they labour in vain that build it
Psalm 127:1 (KJV)

I can imagine God's issue with their plan:

1. *A common people with a common language are puppets and not leaders.*

2. *Centralised government depletes ambition for self governance.*

3. *No matter how benevolent the original dictator may be, centralised government has always led to the rise of a tyrannically leader, even when elected.*

4. *There will be no debate as to right nor wrong, only laws with which men must comply.*

5. *There will be too much room for control and unaccountability.*

6. *The outcome is human secularism.*

7. *The voice of the people will be constrained.*

8. *Unless it is God who wields the power, absolute power corrupts absolutely.*

When weighing all this up, God decided it was time to shut down their system before it went too far.

There is a reason it was called 'Babel' as in Hebrew, Babel means 'confusion'. In modern speech, 'to babble', means to speak confusingly, from which we have the phrase, 'stop babbling'. God confused their language and scattered them throughout the Earth.

So the Lord scattered them from there over all the earth,
and they stopped building the city. That is why it was called
Babel — because there the Lord confused the language of
the whole world. From there the Lord scattered them over
the face of the whole earth.
Genesis 11:8 (NIV)

It would seem then that language is very important to the success of Satan's cosmopolite. People were scattered because they could no longer understand each other! Satan's plans got somewhat hindered and he knew from there it was time to up his strategy. He did this in Egypt. Egypt is Babylon rebranded.

Evolution 2 | The Egyptian model

I can imagine by this time Satan knew that his first cosmopolite had forever been ruined by the language barrier. A challenge he sought to remedy by creating a world where labour and marginal reward could unbeknownst to the polity solicit compliance with little effort.

Then a new king, to whom Joseph meant nothing, came to
power in Egypt. "Look," he said to his people, "the
Israelites have become far too numerous for us. Come, we
must deal shrewdly with them or they will become even
more numerous and, if war breaks out, will join our
enemies, fight against us and leave the country."
Exodus 1:8-10 (NIV)

Notice, there's that word 'shrewd' again. It connotes a sensible wisdom that is often, but not always, instigated by Satan. Here also was that problem again, that they are too numerous to be counted. Egypt up until this time had a bilateral agreement with Israel through Joseph. Joseph's story led Israel (Jacob's house) and Egypt to the height of economic success and established their joint coalition as a superpower in the Earth. Nations flooded Egypt in search for food during a steep recession that, if not for the intervention of God, would have undoubtedly led to the starvation and death of many in the Eastern world.

With Joseph now dead, a new king rose to power who was suspicious of the Israeli's and forgot this bilateral agreement. Through a shrewd spirit, he sought to deal wisely with them. His suspicion unwarranted and obviously Satan charged led him to establish a system that would secure compliance.

Whereas Babylon pursued and exploited sameness of thought and language, Egypt went on to exploit something far more sinister - survival. Babylon was a unified cosmopolitan where people felt a willing desire to work towards a common (although misguided) goal. Egypt, however, became a system where people were motivated by hunger. A classist system was introduced where the truly poor were subjected into forced labour for the truly rich.

True labour is deeply motivating! Economists and sociologists have studied this for centuries and come to the conclusion that people enjoy work! We are motivated by autonomy, mastery and purpose. Autonomy describes the human desire to have control over our own destinies, mastery describes our desire to get better at doing things like playing the piano to improve our skill, whilst purpose describes our desire to have some kind of spiritual vision.

Egypt robbed Israel of its autonomy, mastery and purpose! It turned people into slower more compliant work horses rather than people. It created a false sense of security that if you worked hard you could go home and put food on the table for your family.

Some might argue that this form of government was capitalist, if so it was a very greedy form of capitalism. Capitalism describes private ownership of land and business.

This economic structure gave the workers no rights to private ownership over the means of production, but rather the means of production was entirely owned by the State of Egypt and the people became employees of the State. This structure did not happen overnight but rather overtime. It included the first health system wherein midwives and physicians were forced to perform state sponsored abortions on babies even if it was not complicit with their spiritual beliefs. The eugenics and infanticidal project were likely branded as affordable health care. These late term abortions were a sure way to cull the numbers of those deemed the lowest in Egyptian society, the Israelites.

> The king of Egypt said to the Hebrew midwives, whose names were Shiphrah and Puah, "When you are helping the Hebrew women during childbirth on the delivery stool, if you see that the baby is a boy, kill him; but if it is a girl, let her live."
> Exodus 1:15-16 (NIV)

It would seem as though this plan would work. A society where every individual works for the government and institutions are owned and controlled by government is, from some viewpoints, a credible step towards equality, distribution of wealth and labour. However, what happens when said government goes through austere times? Or if the next leader does not have the same heart and interest as their predecessor, as was the case with this Pharaoh?

What happens when a government has trade deficits or national debt? Does the government pay those debts out of good will or exact on the very people they serve the kind of taxes or labour necessary to boost GDP? Do the people somehow then become the property of the state as well? Do their lives become a guarantee to the lender of restitution?

> *So they put slave masters over them to oppress them with forced labor, and they built Pithom and Rameses as store cities for Pharaoh.*
> *Exodus 1:11 (NIV)*

The government of Egypt set over the Israelites government bosses. These bosses made life very difficult for Israel. It is hard to imagine that they did this deliberately, since many of these task masters were likely to be Israeli's themselves. It would seem again there are many pros and cons to this cosmopolite:

Pros:

1. Government ownership of labour and land means everyone gets a chance to succeed.
2. Government welfare programs means everyone eats and has their basic needs taken care of.
3. Balance of wealth and earnings
4. National infrastructure gets an upgrade
5. Eradication of corporate monopolies
6. Jobs market base
7. Central banks secure wealth

Cons:

1. Higher taxes are demanded.
2. Citizens become entitled and not empowered.
3. Full control is given to government rather than to God.
4. Sectors like health sectors decide the morality of the nation, rather than the church.
5. Where purpose, mastery and autonomy die suicide rates and depression rates increase.
6. When government is in debt, people are held at ransom.
7. The people are ruled by anonymous bureaucrats rather than democratically elected officials.
8. Voices of dissent are not welcome.
9. Central government banks defraud the people of their wealth by debasing currency or increasing interest rates.

The force of social pressure

You might ask yourself, what made these Israelites stay in a place that they were being treated so unfairly? The answer is simple and holds true today! They stayed because everyone else stayed! They simply did what everyone else was doing!

This phenomenon has been increasingly studied in famous experiments like the 1950's Solomon Asch experiment, which explored the relationship between social pressure and conformity.

Asch's experiment was put to 50 college students as a 'vision test' during which the participants were shown a card with a line drawn upon it and a second card showing three lines. The participants were divided into groups and were tasked with identifying which line on the second card most resembled the line on the first card.

The participants were asked to give their answers out loud in the hearing of their group peers. However, within each group, only one unsuspecting participant was the true test subject. Each of the other participants were secretly briefed in advance as to which answer to give and, specifically, to voice the correct answer only for the first 12 tests and to voice the incorrect answer for the final 6 tests. The unsuspecting true test subject was positioned last in line to voice their response. The experiment observed whether the unsuspecting true test subject would conform to the majority group even though it was in blatant error.

Over a series of tests, the findings were that 75% of the true test participants conformed at least one time to those in majority that gave incorrect answers. Only 25% did not conform at all. In a control group when responses were able to be in written form, thus with no peer pressure, only 1% gave incorrect answers.

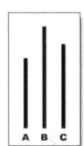

The true test participants were asked why they gave their answers as they did. Most revealed that although they knew the answer was wrong they conformed due to fear of ridicule. Others said they conformed as they believed the majority were correct.

Despite having inherent limitations, the Asch experiment is extremely interesting research and tells us that, apparently, people conform for two main reasons:

1. *They want to fit in with the group (normative influence)*
2. *They believe the group is better informed than themselves (informational influence).*

Coming back to the events described in Exodus, how did Pharaoh achieve Israelite compliance with his regime? It was gained through group influence. Pharoah simply allowed the Israelites to influence themselves! It created a culture of a national minimum wage, central banks and its own National Health service with abortion clinics set in key Israeli communities to ease the swelling population and its demand on Egyptian infrastructure.

Egypt in Hebrew is the word '*Mitsrayim*' which means to limit! The government owned every institution: It owned

1. *The health sector (Exodus 1:15-18)*
2. *The jobs sector (Exodus 1:11,14)*
3. *The monetary sector (Exodus 1:11)*
4. *The means of production (Exodus 1:11)*

In order to truly limit and control the Israelites, the government needed to own one more area of industry.

> *So they put slave masters over them to oppress them with forced labor, and they built Pithom and Rameses as store cities for Pharaoh.*
> *Exodus 1:11*

By owning the banks, the government would have full control over the people. Whereas in the Babylonian cosmopolite there was media control (control of communication) in the Egyptian cosmopolite there was fiscal control (control of economy). The Israelites were financial hostages. Their stocks, bonds and futures were hedged up in the government they now fully served and gave their wealth to. In return they got leaks, onions and the right to eat food everyday provided for them by the government.

The system for the most part worked until God sent a prophet - a voice of dissent, to change the plan! How did God set millions of economic slaves free from a place called limitation?

> *"And I will make the Egyptians favorably disposed toward this people, so that when you leave you will not go empty-handed. Every woman is to ask her neighbor and any woman living in her house for articles of silver and gold and for clothing, which you will put on your sons and daughters. And so you will plunder the Egyptians."*
> *Exodus 3:21-22 (NIV)*

God eradicated Egypt by raiding Pithom and Rameses. In a day, Hebrew slaves received massive reparations and became multi billionaires. Israel traded their silver and gold for leeks and onions. Something that is still happening today and a subject we will discuss in the chapter titled 'Give to Caesar what belongs to Caesar.' But in these two world systems we find Satan's four point global strategy.

Satan's global strategy:

1. *Control Communication - Media*
2. *Control Commerce - Means*
3. *Control Currency - Money*
4. *Control Culture - Meaning*

These four things make up the intellectual property of Satan's kingdom. If the church can become a voice (prophetic) again, we will take back communication, if we can own the means of supply then we could literally establish the Kingdom of Heaven in the Earth. If we can learn how money works then we can see a wealth transfer from the wicked to the righteous and if we can shape the culture, we can release righteousness, peace and joy in the Holy Ghost wherever we are!

Unfortunately, the church by and large has only occupied the communication realm but without taking the other three we will not see a push back of the Kingdom of darkness and an advancing Kingdom of God. The communication realm is the key to the others, but if our theology is right yet our cosmology is wrong, then we will only ever communicate in silo and never cross from church into culture.

Chapter Five

Image is Everything

What Satan is most afraid of!

Image is everything

> *In whom the god of this world hath blinded the minds of*
> *them which believe not, lest the light of the glorious gospel*
> *of Christ, who is the image of God, should shine unto them.*
> *2 Corinthians 4:4 (NIV)*

Satan's ultimate goal is to blind the minds of unbelievers to the image of God! And by unbelievers, I mean Christians too! It is possible to be an unbelieving believer! If so, these unbelieving believers are just as blind as unbelievers.

> *Immediately the boy's father exclaimed, "I do believe; help*
> *me overcome my unbelief!"*
> *Mark 9:24 (NIV)*

A believer who does not believe is an unbeliever and the enemy, Satan has done a wonderful job of convincing us that going to church, praying and reading the Bible makes us Christians. I can bark but I'm no dog, I can sleep in a barn but I'm no cow. The ultimate goal of Christianity is not to improve my church attendance, it is to make me look like Jesus!

Image is everything, and the enemy of our souls is fighting hard to keep us blind to the image of God as if somehow seeing Him will do something to us quite dramatic and life altering. He wants to create something far more cosmetically

93

pleasing than God, even within the church. We call this, the form of godliness.

> Having a form of godliness but denying its power. Have nothing to do with such people.
> 2 Timothy 3:5 (NIV)

All around us, we have famous and well celebrated church services that are cosmetically godly but deny the power of true godliness. Satan wants to keep us from Jesus's image, and God wants to move us ever closer to the Image of Christ. But just why?

> And we know that in all things God works for the good of those who love him, who have been called according to his purpose. For those God foreknew he also predestined to be conformed to the image of his Son,
> Romans 8:28-29 (NIV)

God has a purpose and you have a purpose. Your purpose may be to

1. Step into full-time ministry
2. Change the world
3. Become a music sensation
4. Own a large company of which the Kingdom of God is the beneficiary
5. To change government by becoming a Christian political figure in the mainstream.
6. To become a pastor of a large church.

God's purpose is that you and I be conformed into the image of Christ. So God will use everything in life to conform you to the image of His Son!

If I gave you coffee beans and told you to eat it, you would think it tasted too bitter, if I gave you sugar and told you to eat it, you would think it tasted too sweet, then flour, you would think it tasted too dry, then nuts, you would think it tasted too nutty, butter would taste too buttery! You see, God has a way of meticulously planning to the finest detail every part of your life to bring you into the image of His dear Son and if you taste all of the ingredients He uses to do it in isolation you would think that they were intended for your harm but if you work it all together you have a coffee cake.

When God is designing your life, He allows for sweet seasons, bitter seasons, nutty seasons and dry seasons because He knows that these are all vital ingredients to fulfilling His end purpose; that you and I look like Jesus. If we taste life in isolation, then we won't see what God is doing.

When Joseph was with his father Jacob, we could say that was a sweet season. When he was sold to slavery we could say that was a nutty season. When he was accused of rape we could say that was a sour season. In the prison we could say that was a dry season but when Joseph finally reached the place of his dream, becoming the Prime minister of Egypt, he met his brothers later who thought would hate him and said,

> *You intended to harm me, but God intended it for good to accomplish what is now being done, the saving of many lives.*
> *Genesis 50:20 (NIV)*

I can imagine that at the end of your life, you will be able to say this to those who resisted you and hurt you on the journey. Even family members. In fact, I prophesy to you that those who mistreated you simply misunderstood what God was working in you and at the end they'll have a reason to love you and you'll have a reason to have mercy on them. It takes being in the image of Christ to forgive those who tried to have you killed.

To Joseph, all of life was about being the greatest but to God all of life was about dying to self and becoming like Christ! Satan loves selfish ambition and the rat race to the top! So much so that many of you are frustrated by the lack of opportunity and fulfilled prophetic promise!

I came to announce to you that just like Joseph in the prison season trying to hand out his business card to people, you cannot manipulate your seasons to change! God has you in your season for a reason!

> Then he sent someone to Egypt ahead of them— Joseph, who was sold as a slave. They bruised his feet with fetters and placed his neck in an iron collar. Until the time came to fulfil his dreams, the LORD tested Joseph's character.
> Psalm 105:17-19 (NLT)

Did you see this, until the time came to fulfil his dreams, the Lord tested Joseph's character! God has divinely orchestrated to the finest detail the ingredients that He knows will bring you into the image of Christ. Satan is terrified, not of you achieving your dreams but of you looking like Christ when you get there!

Imagine:

1. *Stepping into full-time ministry with Christ's character (two things that are not mutually inclusive).*
2. *Changing the world looking like Jesus.*
3. *Becoming a music sensation that points to Christ and not to self.*
4. *Owning a large company and looking like Christ, functioning with integrity, providing jobs for the Nation, paying national debts.*
5. *Becoming a politician that looks like Christ and boldly makes decisions not based on popular whim but on moral conviction.*

This is what Satan is afraid of, a 'Jesus Image' generation! He fears it more than anything in this world! He knows that the day you look like Jesus, that he (Satan) is obligated to respect you! But just why?

'I guess smart phones aren't that smart!'

Image consciousness is a great thing! Depending on whose image you are conscious of! When God made you, He made you in His image and after His likeness.

> *Then God said, "Let us make mankind in our image, in our likeness, SO THAT THEY MAY RULE*
> *Genesis 1:26 (NIV)*

Did you see that, 'so that they may rule...' Image is quite simply the only way to have rulership and exercise authority in this world! If you do not look like Jesus, you do not have Jesus rule! Governance is the goal of heaven but only governance that looks like Jesus.

I am an identical twin and I wasn't always so well behaved. My twin and I used to get up to all sorts of mischief. I wasn't always so sporty so my brother would take my sports classes, he wasn't always so brainy so I would take his difficult classes. If he needed my confidence to chat up a girl, I would pretend to be him and if I needed his looks to get a girl, he would gladly give the dreamy eyes to a girl across the room for my sake. The con worked on one proviso, that I used his name! If the teacher called his name and I refused to answer, the gig was up!

Are you getting this? being in my brother's image and mimicking his likeness gave me the same access as my brother had but I had to be fully conscious of his likeness by adopting his name.

You see, all Christianity is, is a big dress rehearsal and we are all meant to be wearing Christ and not a better version of ourselves.

> *And when you were baptised, it was as though you had put on Christ in the same way you put on new clothes.*
> *Galatians 3:27 (CEV)*

One day, my brother bought a brand new iPad complete with facial recognition unlocking. We were in Nigeria doing a conference when one of the volunteers needed to unlock my brothers iPad to give him access to the conference wi-fi. The only problem was that my brother had gone on a long break as he wasn't due to speak for a couple of hours. Just then I had a thought, perhaps being in my brothers image could trick the facial recognition software on the smart device to unlock for me. It turns out the smart device wasn't that smart and it unlocked the moment I looked at it. I hope you're getting my point! I had the same authorisation as my brother because I looked like my brother! Being in his image gave me the same access as him and the same authority as him!

There are many illustrations I could give to further drive this point home. One of my favourite illustrations is an illegal one. I will share this story using fictional characters. Whether or not this is a true story, I will leave to you to speculate! All I can say is seriously, don't try this at home!

A friend of mine had twins called Tim and Tom. They were identical in every way. One day, Tim needed to get on a domestic flight headed for Scotland but he had lost his passport. Realising that a passport was simply an image on a document, Tim asked Tom if he could borrow his passport. After much hesitation, Tom consented in the confidence that Tim would have no issues getting past customs. However, something deeply troubled Tom the next day, and it wasn't his conscience. He realised that if Tim were to travel, it wasn't enough for him to have Tom's passport, he would need to change the name on the ticket to Tom. Tim called the airport immediately and had the name changed! He went to the airport and boarded the plane using Tom's name! When he got to customs, they looked at the image on the passport and looked at Tim and let him through without question.

Again, I won't say if that was a true story or not hehe! I'll leave that to your imagination, or maybe if you catch me in a green room somewhere, I'll whisper it to you. However, I hope you get the point. Those twins realised that a passport was nothing more than an image on a document giving them access to 'pass-a-portal' into another Country. They could not 'pass-the-port' unless the image on the document aligned with the image of the person standing in-between them and the port. Tim had the same access and authority as Tom did provided that he was in the same image and he used the right name!

Image is everything! It's not something, it is the entire point of the Bible. That you and I look into it like a mirror and as it reflects Christ back to us, we are supposed to fully align until we have the same access as the one who authored the Scripture! And that my friends, is the total gospel!

> *For if anyone be a hearer of the word, and not a doer, he is like a man observing his natural face in a* MIRROR: *for he observes himself, goes away, and immediately forgets* WHAT KIND OF MAN HE WAS.
> *James 1:23-24 (NKJ)*

What kind of man are you?
The question all of life is asking you, is not what kind of Christian are you? But What kind of man are you?

When you became born again, you were no longer, 'man kind' nor were you,'woman kind,' you became the original 'kind of man' that God originally intended! A man fully made in the mirror reflection of God!

Therefore if any man be in Christ, he is a new creature: old
things are passed away; behold, all things are become
new.
2 Corinthians 5:17 (KJV)

By reason of being born again (born of the spirit), you have
become the original being God created.

Jesus did not come to restore who was lost! He came to
restore what was lost!

"For the Son of Man has come to save that which was lost.
Matthew 18:11 (KJV)

Notice, He did not refer to Himself as the Son of God but as
the Son of man! Literally meaning, as a son of a pre-fallen
Adamic race, I came to restore that which was lost. The big
question here is, what did man lose that Jesus had to come as
a son of man to restore?

Jesus came to restore the 'Kinds!' Remember, God in Genesis
made 'Kinds.' Plants after their 'kind' creeping things after
their 'kind' and you and I after God's 'kind.'

According to Webster, a kind is:

1. *A group united by common traits or interests*
2. *A specific or recognised variety*
3. *Family lineage*

When you and I were made as man in God's image. We became known as 'the God Kind of man!' When we fell from our Creation (Genesis 1:26) and into our Formation (Genesis 2:7) we became 'man-kind' but not the original kind of man that God originally created!

By reason of being in the image of God, the devil could not tell the difference between Adam and God because they were 'twinning!' They looked exactly the same and so no kind in all creation dared to make a prey out Adam because they could not tell the difference between Adam and the Lord God! He had the same authority as the Author of our faith because He was in the same image! Adam was splitting image of His Father! No lion messed with them, no snake dared to bite them because Adam and the Lord looked exactly the same. If you would believe it, in Genesis 1:26, Adam was made in the image of Jesus who was the express image of God. Genesis means 'The Beginning'

> *In the beginning was the Word, and the Word was with*
> *God, and the Word was God. He was with God in the*
> *beginning. Through him all things were made; without him*
> *nothing was made that has been made. In him was life, and*
> *that life was the light of all mankind.*
> *John 1:1-4 (NIV)*

Jesus was there in the beginning as one of the 'Let Us' that came together to make Adam. Adam was a perfect replica of Jesus, with the same authority as Jesus! However, Adam's job description was different. Jesus rules heaven, Adam rules earth 'as Jesus rules heaven!' Jesus in the garden was not flesh, He like Adam in Genesis 1 was a spirit. How do we know this because the scripture goes on to say that for our benefit that just like Adam became flesh, so Jesus became flesh.

> *The Word became flesh and made his dwelling among us.*
> *John 1:14 (NIV)*

If He became flesh, then He wasn't flesh in Genesis. Adam and Jesus were vested with the exact same authority! One was the ruler of heaven, the other was the ruler of earth. The ruler of earths job was to rule earth as it is ruled by Jesus in heaven. This is why, from the moment Jesus created Adam in His image, He (Jesus) never named creation again! He brought them to Adam to see what He would name them!

> *Now the LORD God had formed out of the ground all the wild animals and all the birds in the sky. He brought them to the man TO SEE WHAT HE WOULD NAME THEM; and whatever the man called each living creature, that was its name.*
> *Genesis 2:19 (NIV)*

Every created thing (Genesis 1) God brought the formed thing to Adam to see something! He was trying to see if Adam in Genesis 2 would call them what God already named them in Genesis 1! 'On earth as it is in heaven!' Whatever Adam called it, the Lord God had already named it! This is why faith is:

> *And calleth those things which be not as though they were.*
> *Romans 4:17 (KJV)*

Because Adam was the 'God kind of man,' He literally had the mind of Christ. He named everything in this realm what God already called it in His realm, perfectly. He called into being things which be not as though they pre-existed and somehow exited that realm into this earth realm.

Being in the Image of God gives you and I the ability to call 'formed' things what God called them when He originally created them. They may be deFORMED, wrongly inFORMED or desperately in need of a reFORM but when we declare what it was originally created to be, we can transFORM it into what God called it in heaven 'on Earth as it is in heaven!'

> *By faith we understand that the universe was CREATED*
> *by the word of God, so that what is seen was not made out*
> *of things that are visible.*
> *Hebrews 11:3 (ESV)*

'What is' doesn't matter, 'what was' does! See faith is calling 'what was' as though 'it is!' The universe was created long before the world was formed! Things may look a little deformed but you can still like Adam call out its creation and not its form.

Adam was perfectly made in the image of God! He could see a form and speak perfectly to its creation because Adam knew no one after the flesh! He saw perfectly with the eyes of the spirit!

> *From now on, therefore, we regard no one according to the*
> *flesh.*
> *2 Corinthians 5:16 (ESV)*

Adam called forth their image and not their form! Every kind is an image of another kind and this is why we call them kinds. They have subtle differences, but they are of the same kind. Kinds are very important because what kind of person you think you are determines what kind of results you see!

> For as he thinks in his heart, so is he
> Proverbs 23:7 (NKJV)

Simply put, you are who you think you are! The pivot between the flesh (form) and the spirit (image) is where you put your mind!

> For they that are after the flesh do mind the things of the flesh; but they that are after the Spirit the things of the Spirit.
> Romans 8:5 (KJV)

When you set your mind on the Spirit then you dominate the flesh and its sinful desires. Your meditation therefore is your habitation. The question is, what Kind of man are you?

One day, Jesus and his disciples were on a boat. A storm broke out on the boat and all they that were on it began to be in peril for their own lives except for one man. Jesus! He simply slept through the storm. One of Jesus' disciples mistook his calmness for carelessness and said,

> Master, carest thou not that we perish?
> Mark 4:38 (KJV)

Jesus got up from His pillow and rebuked the winds and spoke to the waves to be quiet then the Bible says that suddenly the wind died down and all was completely calm. I like Matthews version of the question that immediately ensued Jesus calming the waves. It is a most fitting question and indeed it is the question upon which the whole gospel tilts. It is the question that truly gives us hope that we can win this fight against the devil!

> *What kind of man is this?*
> *Matthew 8:27 (NIV)*

Jesus was the Kind that God originally intended us to be. 'the God kind' We lost our kind and Jesus came to restore us back to our kind. Not to a church but to a Person! Not to have an international ministry but to be the original man that could speak to the cosmos and watch it shift right before our eyes!

Till this day, the whole earth is groaning for those sons who can speak to the cosmos and watch creation come into alignment with the will of God the Creator. These sons are made in the Image of God and so they can speak to creation and creation will respond because it does not know the difference between them and God.

> *For the creation waits with eager longing for the revealing*
> *of the sons of God.*
> *Romans 8:19 (RSV)*

Creation has seen pastors, prophets, apostles, evangelists and teachers but it is still waiting eagerly to see those who can speak to creation itself and tell it what to do! Creation will shift the cosmos if you will only learn to speak to it and call forth those things that be not as though they were.

In essence Hebrews 11 says through faith we understand that the universe was made from the realm of the spirit before it ever was ruled by Satan so things that are in the cosmos originated in some form from creativity that can only be found in the spirit! In order to reclaim the cosmos we must raise an army of creatives again! Sonship is the key to creativity! It aligns us with heavenly images so that we can form them in the earth.

The god class!

Satan is not terrified of the day you and I arrive at our destiny, he is terrified of the day we arrive at our image. The church truly arrives when it is in the image of Jesus Christ. The image of Jesus is the only image that Satan is absolutely terrified of and any one in His 'Kind' is a threat. If you are cosmetically in His image but not actually in His image then you are a no better than a Pharisee.

> "Woe to you, teachers of the law and Pharisees, you hypocrites! You are like whitewashed tombs, which look beautiful on the outside but on the inside are full of the bones of the dead and everything unclean.
> Matthew 23:27 (NIV)

Whilst cosmetics are a necessary end which we will discuss later, if cosmetics replaces power then the church becomes performative and not transformative. This was a dimension of understanding that the Apostle Paul attained to where in Galatians 2:20 He says

I have been crucified with Christ and I no longer live, but Christ lives in me. The life I now live in the body, I live by faith in the Son of God, who loved me and gave Himself for me.
Galatians 2:20 (NIV)

We have taught you wrong that Satan is after your end, the truth is he's after your beginning. It is not even your identity that he is fighting for, nor is it your character but your image!

Is character important, absolutely! But not as important as image! The right image will get you in a second where the right character can't get you in a lifetime! Whilst character has its place in our Christian walk, this life truly is a dress rehearsal and not as complex as our theologians and Sunday pastors have made it out to be.

Growing up my twin brother and I started to notice some subtle differences. He became extremely sporty and I for a while excelled in math and spelling at which he was not the most proficient. We learnt quite early on that looking like each other gave us access to one another's classes and that all we simply had to do was answer in the affirmative when one another's name was called. Our teachers only other way of distinguishing us was our ties. In our school we were broken into houses and each house had a unique gradient colour difference in their tie and our headmaster ensured that my brother and I were in different houses purely for identification purposes. So if we wanted to switch classes all we need to do was wear different colour ties.

You see, I had access to his class simply by reason of looking like him, calling his name and changing my disguise. One day he deployed the same tactic to dating my girlfriend who was oblivious to our differences and so he would ask to borrow my tie unbeknownst to me so that he could seek the affection of my unassuming girlfriend. The point is, our character wasn't right but our image was!

Because of his image, he could access everything that belonged to me and I in turn could access everything that belonged to him. Being in God's image gives you access to the God class, this is not dependent on character, but simply on image.

The perfect analogy of this can be found in the story of Isaac and his twin boys in Genesis 27. The blessing was about to be given to Esau the twin brother of Jacob. Isaac who was blind at the time because of old age told Esau to go fetch him venison so that his soul could bless him. Whilst Esau was off preparing it, his brother Jacob gets some wool and puts it on his arms at the advice of his mother Rebekah. Esau was hairy and that was the way Isaac could differentiate them. So by disguising himself and answering to his brother's name the Bible goes on to say that Jacob stole the blessing of Esau. By the time Esau came in it was too late. Isaac, realising that he had been deceived, said this:

> *"Who was it then that hunted game and brought it to me? I ate it just before you came and I blessed him — and indeed he will be blessed?"*
> *Genesis 27:33 (NIV)*

So God allowed Jacob to be blessed even though he deceitfully stole a blessing that did not belong to him? Yes, because righteousness is not right living but right standing!

> *Jacob I have loved, Esau I have hated*
> *Romans 9:13 (NIV)*

You see Esau was busy trying to live right, and all Jacob needed to do was stand right! The one who stands right will always trump the one who tries to live right.

How is it that Saul never committed adultery, spared a king, kept some sheep alive, showed himself to be benevolent and yet God in 1 Samuel 15 calls him stubborn and a witch?

Yet David

1. Slept with another man's wife
2. Got the girl pregnant
3. Killed the woman's husband
4. Married the widow he created
5. Burnt an offering and went into the holy place (a place only permitted for the high priest)

Yet God looked and says, 'man after my own heart'?

> *But now your (Saul's) kingdom will not endure; the Lord has sought a man after His own heart and appointed him ruler over His people.*
> *1 Samuel 13:14 (NIV)*

This is the secret Satan does not want you to know! You can never live right if you don't stand right! Everything you do will become religious and self-righteous. You will become so rigid in your Christian walk that God can't use you anywhere other than in your local church intercessory team. Whoever does what is right is righteous, not whoever does what is good!

> Dear children, do not let anyone lead you astray. The one who does what is right is righteous, just as He is righteous.
> 1 John 3:7 (NIV)

I am not advocating for bad character. I am saying that what we have called bad character is often bad church optics and succumbing to the peer pressure of the form of godliness that has no power. Do good, but never mistake good for right. When we talk about the story of the prodigal son, we spend far too much time in our messages on the prodigal and not enough time on the older brother. For those who don't know the story, here it is below.

> "A certain man had two sons. And the younger of them said to his father, 'Father, give me the portion of goods that falls to me.' So he divided to them his livelihood. And not many days after, the younger son gathered all together, journeyed to a far country, and there wasted his possessions with prodigal living. But when he had spent all, there arose a severe famine in that land, and he began to be in want.
>
> Then he went and joined himself to a citizen of that country, and he sent him into his fields to feed swine. And he would

*gladly have filled his stomach with the pods that the swine
ate, and no one gave him anything.*

*"But when he came to himself, he said, 'How many of my
father's hired servants have bread enough and to spare,
and I perish with hunger! I will arise and go to my father,
and will say to him, "Father, I have sinned against heaven
and before you, and I am no longer worthy to be called
your son. Make me like one of your hired servants." '*

*"And he arose and came to his father. But when he was still
a great way off, his father saw him and had compassion,
and ran and fell on his neck and kissed him. And the son
said to him, 'Father, I have sinned against heaven and in
your sight, and am no longer worthy to be called your son.'*

*"But the father said to his servants, 'Bring out the best robe
and put it on him, and put a ring on his hand and sandals
on his feet. And bring the fatted calf here and kill it, and let
us eat and be merry; for this my son was dead and is alive
again; he was lost and is found.' And they began to be
merry.*

*"Now his older son was in the field. And as he came and
drew near to the house, he heard music and dancing. So
he called one of the servants and asked what these things
meant. And he said to him, 'Your brother has come, and
because he has received him safe and sound, your father
has killed the fatted calf.'*

*"But he was angry and would not go in. Therefore his
father came out and pleaded with him. So he answered
and said to his father, 'Lo, these many years I have been*

serving you; I never transgressed your commandment at
any time; and yet you never gave me a young goat, that I
might make merry with my friends. But as soon as this son
of yours came, who has devoured your livelihood with
harlots, you killed the fatted calf for him.'

"And he said to him, 'Son, you are always with me, and all
that I have is yours. It was right that we should make merry
and be glad, for your brother was dead and is alive again,
and was lost and is found.'"
Luke 15:11-32 (NKJV)

Think about this story! One son went to spend all his father's money, whilst the older son stayed in his father's house, seeming to be living right! He was angry because for all his right living versus his brothers riotous living, his father never gave him so much as a young goat; but the lost son who slept with prostitutes and lived a decadent life got the fattest calf, a ring and a robe. Why? Because righteousness has nothing to do with right living, but rather, right standing. You can live in the father's house and get so comfortable in your religious righteous rags and still not be in right standing.

The greatest danger of our time is that we have conformed many people to church but very few to Christ. The complaint of the older son was that he had been serving and yet the answer of the father was to remind him that he was not a servant, he was a son and sons have access that servants don't have!

You love your son, no matter how naughty he is, you do him good because he is your son, servant mentality will make you serve for God's approval instead of serving from God's approval.

The father covered him in a robe. Why? Because the robe represents the covering of Jesus.

> *He has covered me with the robe of righteousness*
> *Isaiah 61:10 (NKJV)*

According to the dictionary to cover means to conceal something illicit, blameworthy or embarrassing from notice or to place under concealment. When Jesus died for you and you clothed yourself with Him, the enemy couldn't tell the difference between you and Jesus.

Jesus doesn't need your righteousness; He's got you covered! Purity is not what you do for Him, purity is what you do for you to stay in right standing with Him. You don't depreciate in God's eyes, but when you sin you depreciate in your own eyes and it takes you longer to return to your Father's house.

This life is a dress rehearsal and we are all called to put off ourselves and to put on Jesus!

> *Rather clothe yourselves with the Lord Jesus Christ, and do*
> *not think about how to gratify the desires of the flesh*
> *Romans 13:14 (NIV)*

Don't be like the elder brother, so conformed to church that He was not conformed to Christ! 'Fathers house' mentality will do that to you and in doing so, you become ineffective in a world so in need of a touch from heaven.

Chapter Six
Culture!
From escaping the global cult to changing it

Redefining Culture
In 1986, philosopher Edward S Casey wrote,

> *"The very word culture meant 'place tilled' in Middle English, and the same word goes back to Latin colere, 'to inhabit, care for, till, worship and cultus, 'A cult, especially a religious one.'*

Yes, in Satan's cosmos there are many cults but the biggest of them all is culture! Culture is the culmination of a range of phenomena transmitted by and large through social learning as opposed to institutional learning. It is not codified, nor is it at first ratified into any common, constitutional, national or international law but it manages to exist as unwritten rules embedded in the fabric of society passed down through tradition from one person to another.

Many Christians are taught that culture is dangerous, but however terrible culture may be, there are both redeemable and irredeemable qualities in every culture.

'To culture' comes from a word meaning 'to cultivate'. Each day of our Christian lives, God is expecting us to cultivate the land we live in to make it more like God intended. It is why Adam was formed. Adam was to cultivate the ground on behalf of God.

Culture shapers

You can never change a culture that you have subscribed to. In order to change the culture, you must first learn to recognise that at its base composition, culture is made up of airtight, interwoven threads of rules and traditions of men that demand compliance. These rules and traditions are known as 'norms' or 'normative behaviour'.

You know you are being cultured when what was normative behaviour yesterday has expanded its definition overnight and a new rule is demanding compliance. These rules and traditions are socially educated so-called norms set by 'culture shapers' who are forever redefining the boundaries of the concept of 'norm.'

The culture shapers of the cosmos world have become 'celebrities'. This makes the prospect of you or I being a culture shaper feel daunting and at times futile. After all, their mass following is their superpower and they have spent a lot of time and money to cultivate that.

Most people measure influence by one's platform and when looking at the seemingly Goliath size culture shapers operating in every field – the arts, business, government, education, news media and even the church – can feel dwarfed by them and worry that their own voice will never be heard.

History is replete with men and women who challenged 'the establishment' from Michael Jackson who popularised a whole new genre of music and was the reason MTV had its success and even creation; to Martin Luther who challenged the Roman Catholic Church when he placed the 95th Thesis on the All Saints Church in Germany, declaring that we are saved by grace and not through a priest nor catholic sacrament, thus birthing the protestant movement; and Rosa Parks who became the most iconic civil rights female leader of our lifetime by refusing to sit in a segregationist seat on a bus. I could go on to talk about great men and great women who achieved great feats and became the figures we now herald as celebrities, but although they be celebrated now, many of these and women were hated whilst they were alive.

Culture disruptors

Anyone who challenges the culture and does not want to be hated is simply not ready to challenge the culture! When Jesus called for twelve disciples, he was really calling for twelve disrupters, who he could refashion to disrupt the cosmos (world order, orderly arrangement). It was said of these cosmopolitan Christians in that day,

> But when they did not find them, they dragged Jason and some brethren to the rulers of the city, crying out, "These who have turned the world upside down have come here too..."
> Acts 17:6 (NLKV)

Another translation says,

> '...these men who have caused trouble all over the world have now come here.
> Acts 17:6 (NIV)

What a powerful statement! Christians used to be known as disruptors not conformers! A Christian will disrupt Satan's kingdom whether that be in the church, the stock market, the criminal system or the classist system. When the Church is on the scene, the order gets flipped, or so it should.

According to Merriam a disrupter is anyone who interrupts the normal course or unity of something. Nobody likes a disrupter, especially Satan. Order is how he keeps everyone, including the church in check. The devil is highly organised and deeply synergised with the patterns of culture itself. He is so unobtrusive that the world is by and large oblivious to his assignment or indeed his existence.

Learning to break the rules and traditions

The taskmasters that keep most people in check today are nothing more than rules and traditions. Anyone who is celebrated today found a rule worth breaking and they broke it!

> "Leadership is the ability to find a rule worth breaking and then breaking it!" (Dr Myles Munroe)

Jesus put it like this,

> And in vain they worship Me, Teaching as doctrines the commandments of men.' For laying aside the commandment of God, you hold the tradition of men—the washing of pitchers and cups, and many other such things you do." He said to them, "All too well you reject the commandment of God, that you may keep your tradition. For Moses said, 'Honour your father and your mother'; and, 'He who curses father or mother, let him be put to death.' But you say, 'If a man says to his father or mother, "Whatever profit you might have received from me is Corban"—' (that is, a gift to God), then you no longer let

him do anything for his father or his mother, making the
word of God of no effect through your tradition which you
have handed down. And many such things you do."
Mark 7:7-13 (NKJV)

God's Word Translation says,

Their worship of me is pointless, because their teachings
are rules made by humans.'
Mark 7:7 (GW)

Their worship is pointless because they teach rules as if they
were Biblical teachings. The word of God which has power to
transform nations is ineffective because the church has been
conditioned to follow all the rules. Once someone breaks the
rules in church there is someone there to put them back in
their place. Christ calls us all to break the rules by being the
first example in every way of a rule breaker!

Let's take a look at the rules that Jesus broke.

Rule 1 - Do not touch a leper

A man with leprosy came and knelt before him and said,
"Lord, if you are willing, you can make me clean." Jesus
reached out his hand and touched the man. "I am willing,"
he said. "Be clean!" Immediately he was cleansed of his
leprosy.
Matthew 8:2-3 (NIV)

In those days, you were not allowed to come into the
community if you possessed leprosy. According to tradition,
you got the illness because you deserved it. Anyone who

touched an unclean person, especially being a priest was considered unclean.

By touching the leper Jesus broke the rules and was thus considered full of sin to anyone who would have seen him do so.

Rule 2 – Always observe ceremonial washing

According to tradition, washing up to the elbows was mandatory before eating. This included ceremoniously baptising what you will eat with. Jesus broke that rule knowing fully well that it was a generally accepted custom.

> *Now when the Pharisees and some of the scribes who had come from Jerusalem gathered around him, they noticed that some of his disciples were eating with defiled hands, that is, without washing them. (For the Pharisees, and all the Jews, do not eat unless they thoroughly wash their hands, thus observing the tradition of the elders;*
> *Mark 7:1-3 (NRSV)*

Rule 3 – Do not eat with sinners

According to tradition you were not supposed to be seen eating and sitting with the world. Jesus broke the rule.

> *And as he sat at dinner in Levi's house, many tax collectors and sinners were also sitting with Jesus and his disciples — for there were many who followed him.*
> *Mark 2:15 (NRSV)*

Rule 4 – Do not heal on the Sabbath

According to tradition, the Sabbath was a day to do nothing and to be idle. Jesus constantly broke the rules by healing on the Sabbath day.

> *Another time Jesus went into the synagogue, and a man with a shriveled hand was there. Some of them were looking for a reason to accuse Jesus, so they watched him closely to see if he would heal him on the Sabbath. Jesus said to the man with the shriveled hand, "Stand up in front of everyone."*
>
> *Then Jesus asked them, "Which is lawful on the Sabbath: to do good or to do evil, to save life or to kill?" But they remained silent. He looked around at them in anger and, deeply distressed at their stubborn hearts, said to the man, "Stretch out your hand." He stretched it out, and his hand was completely restored. Then the Pharisees went out and began to plot with the Herodians how they might kill Jesus. Mark 3:1-6 (NIV)*

I could go on to talk about how Jesus forgave sins and let a prostitute clean his feet with her tears at the dinner table of Israel's most elite leaders. However, my point is this, that the reason we all know Jesus today is not because of how well he conformed, but by how much He disrupted the order. The wooly, Hollywood Jesus that is worshipped today is not the rule breaking, heretic Messiah of the Scripture!

Hero heretics

When it comes to apostolic ministry, you are only as successful as the rules you're willing to break and the risks you're willing to take! Nobody standing in will ever stand out!

> *"You are the light of the world—like a city on a hilltop that cannot be hidden.*
> *Matthew 5:14 (NLT)*

Standing out in a kosmos that has pressured us into conformity is difficult, but heroes are born when they refuse to conform! We later call these heroes heretics.

> *It is enough for the disciple that he be as his master, and the servant as his lord. If they have called the master of the house Beelzebub, how much more shall they call them of his household?*
> *Matthew 10:25 (KJV)*

It all begins in the home!

I start with the home because the family is the birthing ground of change and contrary to popular opinion, the parents are the first heroes and culture setters before school, media, entertainment, gang culture and government take over. Parents are the future of this global transformative effort as all rules and traditions begin in the home.

You may not be a parent but believe me, this chapter will save you a lot of heart ache one day when, or if indeed, you do decide to raise your own children or become responsible for the next generation in any way shape or form.

Traditions and rules are like invisible strings being pulled by an invisible puppet master. People are obligated to follow things that the only consequence of violating is humanistic and involves peer and family pressure to conform. Peter and the other apostles responded to this pressure with:

> "We must obey God rather than human beings!
> Acts 5:29 (NIV)

I'll never forget the story my twin brother shared at a conference in Lagos, Nigeria that had us all in tears. Our family moved to the UK when my brother and I were two years old and so we grew up very much in a Western culture, but was raised entirely by parents who held fast to their African culture and indeed their traditions. During his preach, my brother recounted the time he came home from school feeling rather 'Western' in his outlook (dare I say, rebellious). He had seen many of the English kids talk back to their parents with shocking informality and have such strong disagreements with them, even in some cases insulting them. Whilst my brother wasn't brave enough to insult my mother, he was brave enough to question her on whether or not he should leave till later what my mum was insisting be done right away. You see, in Africa, an instruction given by one's parent is assumed to require immediate execution, without the need for the parent to say 'do it now'. It is normal for the kid to jump up from the moment the parent enters the room and there is no tolerance whatsoever for backchat. My brother stood up and sheepishly told my mum,

"This is England, mum, we don't have to do all that here!"

He must have immediately known that he had messed up when my mum grabbed him by his face, took him to the living room window and pressed his nose into it with enough force to smudge his nose and cheek against the cold England window. She exclaimed in her strong African intonation,

"Son, make no mistake, out there is England, but inside this house is Africa!"

Suffice to say, my brother never did that again.

We were raised very much in the African culture, even though we were in the UK. In fact, when we went back to Nigeria almost 28 years later to preach, crowds were actually quite amazed at the Nigerian parental nuances that we understood so well. They would often ask how we know Nigeria so well having not lived there so long and our response would always be the same,

"We were born in Nigeria, but assembled in England."

Rules and traditions are not geographical, they are deeply spiritual. Just as with my family, these ancestral ideologies, advanced by unknown spiritual forces, can traverse the geographical parameters set for them.

For three years, I was the leader of an ethnically diverse church in Windsor, United Kingdom. During that time, I observed how my European congregants would parent their children mostly through the lens of love, whilst my African and Asian congregants would parent mostly through the lens of respect. Both these parenting styles had their roots in their respective ethnic traditions.

Tradition comes from the word 'trade'. It is the transmission of ideas, concepts and ways of life through learned behaviours. It is very difficult to erase these learned behaviours and most parents who wish to break away from the traditions within which they were raised find it extremely challenging. This is especially evident during times of high stress when involuntary responses, both in the words or behaviour patterns of one's parents come bellowing out! Tradition is ancestral and coming against it means violating centuries of tradition.

My dad's parents died when he was fifteen years old. He was almost entirely self-raised and self-taught and became a medical doctor and now a consultant general practitioner due to sheer hard work and self-discipline. Despite losing his parents whilst still very young, his parenting style was heavily influenced by the first fifteen years he had with them. For example, he would say things like,

> *"I never spoke to my father like that, so you will never speak to me like that."*

It wasn't until my father met Jesus that he realised that these were statements of fear and based entirely on losing a code that he was no longer beholden to.

Many of us fall prey to tradition and the rules handed down from our parents, grandparents and other ancestors who may no longer alive today. The result of this indebtedness is almost always entirely devastating. Why? Because no one child or generation is the same. The enforcement of tradition and ancestral rules upon a child is a form of bulk production parenting that puts parents in factory mode, reproducing clones instead of well-rounded children. I now greatly sympathise and empathise with my father's plight back in those early years, because being a parent myself, I now understand the pressure and stress. It is extremely easy to turn on bulk-parenting mode when there are bills to pay and thankless mouths to feed, but in doing so, the uniqueness of each child is neglected along with the relationship.

Once in a generation a parent will go off script and choose to do the opposite of what they were taught and this too has its challenges. A parent raised in a home of verbal or physical abuse might determine to opt for the kind, loving and non-physical approach to discipline, but then God gives them a child that is abrasive, extroverted and daring. My point is, rebelling against ancestral spirits often comes with just as many consequences as following them.

Rules! Rules! Rules!

The rules of my house when growing up can be pretty much summed up as.

> *Go to school, get a good education, graduate (with honours) go to university, get a degree (in medicine, law, engineering) then get a good job with good benefits and then get married.*

When you look at the root of all rules they are embedded in fear. The fear of children rebelling, the fear of children misbehaving, the fear of children leaving you. The fact is that all rules will eventually be broken and they will be adhered to for a while but eventually the end of every rule is rebellion.

The reason kids are leaving the home to join gangs or are truanting at school or acting out is quite simply because there are just too many rules. If you want to raise the next generation of cosmopolitan Christians, you have to throw out all the rules. Not some of them, but all of them!

I can already see a parent's right eye twitching at this statement. We have been wrongly taught to raise our children to follow the rules. When they defiantly ask why, the universal answer is, 'Because I'm your parent and I told you to do it, so do it!' The truth is, however, the reason we answer like this is because there are no valid reasons whatsoever to follow the rules.

You may think that you have mastered this discipline thing and created an underage sex free, drug free, rebellion free home, but the truth is you have created a ticking time bomb. Where there is no 'why' there is only 'when!' Most kids can't wait to leave the house because they know that when they leave they will be free of your rules and able to do all the things you said they couldn't do because you never gave them a sufficient 'why'. If you were to tell them the truth as to why they had to follow your rules it would sound something like this,

> *'Because I am terrified of you repeating my mistakes and being disappointed like I was.'*

Or

*'Because I am afraid to death of losing you to someone
else. I would rather keep you and you hate me than lose
you and you love me.'*

Or

'I was just trying to protect you!'

The list could go on, but nowhere in the Bible are we told to
raise our children to follow rules. In fact, if you want to raise
failures in life, then teach them how to follow the rules.

The problem with bulk-parenting mode is that whilst the
demand is constantly changing, the factory keeps running the
same supply chain. In essence, the rules are always changing
and so every parent must know that the rules they are handing
down to their children are at least 20 years out of date. Why?
Because every twenty years a new generation is born and with
each generation there is a new song to be played, a new
sermon to be written, a new way to live. Tradition and rules
eventually lead to rebellion because no parent teaches their
children that the rules quite simply 'suck!' Just like the prodigal
son, somehow the child who followed them all their life always
ends up worse off than the one who breaks all of them. The
rules are always changing and what worked yesterday no
longer works today. Our school text books are dramatically out
of date, our whole way of living is in desperate need of an
overhaul and in another twenty years it will do the same
revolution. Every revolution is led by someone young enough
and naive enough to break all the rules.

Bill Gates, in the 90's, was every 'Generation-Xers' rule
breaker. He was a pain to his parents and never followed their

rules. Finally, he got to go to Harvard University only to drop out to start what would later be known as Microsoft! Microsoft was created by a rule breaker! Rule breakers are by the very definition of the word, leaders! So maybe you don't have a rebellious child, perhaps you have a frustrated leader who knows your rules don't work in his day. Maybe like Saul to David all you are really doing to help them is harming them.

> *Then Saul clothed David with his garments and put a bronze helmet on his head, and he clothed him with armour. David girded his sword over his armour and tried to walk, for he had not tested them. So David said to Saul, "I cannot go with these, for I have not tested them." And David took them off.1 Samuel 17:38-39 (NASB)*

Can you imagine how arrogant David looked in the midst of an experienced war veteran like Saul. Saul was prescribing rules to a rule breaker. Prescribing rules to a rule breaker is always perceived as rejection and breaking the rules of a rule follower is always perceived as rebellion. The curse of rule following all begins in the family! Someone told us that we had to raise kids that followed rules. So just how do we raise our kids?

Laws! Laws! Laws!

If you are going to raise a cosmopolitan Christian that does not compromise on truth and is in the cosmos but not of the cosmos then you must begin to understand laws.

Seven things you need to know about Laws by the late Dr Myles Munroe:

1. Laws are predictive indicators of success.

2. Embedded in every law is its own consequence for violating it.
3. Laws are universal, unquestionable and ageless.
4. The ultimate consequence of violating laws is death and the executioner of every law violated is the law in itself.
5. Laws are divine and put in place by the wisdom of the Creator for order and for protection.
6. Laws are written.
7. The end of every law followed is success.

Seven things you need to know about Rules:

1. Rules are predictive indicators of failure.
2. Rules have no consequences except peer pressure for violating them.
3. Rules are traditional, questionable and age like a curry left on a cold stove.
4. The ultimate consequence of violating rules is mob justice and the executioner of every rule violated are the thought leaders within that rule
5. Rules are human and put in place by parents, society and eventually peer groups, All of whom assume they are wise.
6. Rules are assumed.
7. The end of every rule followed is rebellion.

Jesus said, the mistake we are making is three fold:

1. Violating the laws of God

For you ignore God's law and substitute your own tradition.

Mark 7:8 (NLT)

2. Teaching rules as if they were laws

    They worship me in vain, teaching as doctrines human commands.
    Mark 7:7 (CSB)

3. Making the word of God ineffective

    making the word of God of no effect through your tradition which you have handed down. And many such things you do."
    Mark 7:13 (NKJV)

When you make rules into laws then you raise children who eventually rebel or live their whole lives like a broken computer program that processes life wrongly and outputs all the wrong information to a world where the rules are always changing.

Rules are what computer programs are made from. Rules computerise a generation. The problem is, children are not silicon chips that you can just upload your favourite software two and upgrade every now and again to the latest operating system. If we raise children like this, they will get married and have children off of the last operating system you gave them perhaps when they were eighteen. Most married couples are like eighteen year olds in adult bodies trying to figure out why the rules of their upbringing are ruining their marriage. Then you get the mammas boys who always go back to mamas house because she's the only one that can upgrade the operating system but she loves the dependency too much to upgrade him so she'll put some tweaks to him enough to keep him coming home for shepherds pie.

Laws help us succeed; rules help us fail

The Bible is a Book of irrefutable divine laws that if you take the time to meditate on, you will find the secrets of success.

> *This Book of the Law shall not depart from your mouth, but you shall meditate in it day and night, that you may observe to do according to all that is written in it. For then you will make your way prosperous, and then you will have good success.*
> *Joshua 1:8 (NKJV)*

The sad thing is, most people in our generation are leaving the church because it is no longer teaching the laws of God, but rather the rules of man.

In fact, in most cases, whilst the church is teaching rules, the Kosmos is teaching laws. Many Christians today have Tony Robbins as their virtual pastor of choice and their local church pastor as their supplemental religious itch scratching option. Why is this? Because Tony Robbins may be swearing every five minutes, but he is teaching laws. God embeds His divine laws within every human being.

> *Indeed, when Gentiles [sinners], who do not have the law, do by nature things required by the law, they are a law for themselves, even though they do not have the law.*
> *Romans 2:14 (NIV)*

Laws are God's wisdom to us.

See, I have taught you decrees and laws as the LORD my
God commanded me, so that you may follow them in the
land you are entering to take possession of it.
Observe them carefully, for this will show your wisdom and
understanding to the nations, who will hear about all these
decrees and say, "Surely this great nation is a wise and
understanding people."
Deuteronomy 4:5-6 (NIV)

*When we leave laws behind, we leave the wisdom of God
behind*

While the church distances itself from God's laws in pursuit of
relevance, in fact the opposite is happening and we are no
longer respected by a Kosmos that acknowledges the inherent
wisdom of those laws, but refusing to acknowledge God, has
been repackaging and rebranding God's laws as *'laws of the
universe.'*

The only law we are no longer under is the law of sin and
death. The ceremonial law was taken care of in Christ's death
on the cross.

He did not enter by the blood of goats and calves, but He
entered the Most Holy Place once for all by His own blood,
thus securing eternal redemption. The blood of goats and
bulls and the ashes of a heifer sprinkled on those who are
ceremonially unclean sanctify them so that they are
outwardly clean. How much more, then, will the blood of
Christ, who through the eternal Spirit offered Himself
unblemished to God, cleanse our consciences from acts
that lead to death, so that we may serve the living God!

Hebrews 9:12-14 (NIV)

Not even Jesus could break the law of sin and death, even He had to fulfil it in His death on the Cross, because laws cannot be broken, they can only be fulfilled. When the writer of the law dies then and only then can new laws be made, or in our case a New Covenant.

> *Think not that I am come to destroy the law, or the prophets: I am not come to destroy, but to fulfil.*
> *Matthew 5:17 (KJV)*

The law of the fish is the water. It is not a rule, it is a law! If the fish is to survive it must be taught the law of the water. If the fish tries to break the law of the water, then the law will break the fish.

The law of you and I is the presence of God. If we try to break this law then this law will break us. Every law has consequences imbedded within the law itself to keep us from violating it. For the fish that leaves the water, the consequence is suffocation. For the plant that leaves the soil, it is withering. For you and I leaving the presence of God, it is a fruitless life.

> *Remain in Me, and I will remain in you. Just as the branch cannot bear fruit by itself, unless it remains in the vine, so neither can you unless you remain in Me.*
> *John 15:4 (NET)*

Rules are not so! A rule of your church maybe that only important people sit at the front of the church and every time the pastor shows up you bow! Whilst I am not averse to customs, they must remain just that, customs! If these become laws, then control sets into the church very quickly and the end of all control is rebellion.

I would love to spend more time exploring the difference between rules and laws, but it is not the purpose of this book and I do not wish to go off topic. I strongly suggest you download my app by searching 'RIG Nation' in my app store for a more in-depth teaching in this area.

Disobeying honourably

Culture and tradition are held together by ancestral spirits that are enshrined into every cultures humanities and arts to ensure that they never change. These spirits often leave the paintings that adorn our museums to enter into guardians of tradition. These guardians of today are not as smart as their more theological historic counterparts such as the pharisees. Rather, they have smart phones and Twitter accounts which makes them even more dangerous.

Sentimentality is why we embed these familiar spirits in our arts and humanities so deeply that anyone who dares question them is seen as non-patriotic or heretical. To challenge the status quo is the very objective of the 'Cosmopolitan Christian'. I hope you understand that this is not about raising a vandalistic generation that hates all tradition, but rather it is about raising a law-abiding generation who have laws within themselves that will force them to violate rules in order to follow God's law.

God's law says honour your father and mother in Ephesians 6:2, but if read in isolation, this Scripture can easily become a rule rather than a law of success. This is because the very first verse has a clause that most parents do not quote to their children.

> *Children, obey your parents* IN THE LORD, *for this is right.*
> *Ephesians 6:1*

The law of success for children is to obey parents in the Lord! When parents tell you to do something outside of the Lord then it is not a violation of God's law to disobey the instruction. It is however a violation of God's law to disobey it dishonourably. We can disobey honourably!

I will never forget meeting a grown woman in her late thirties who had never been married because her mum did not like any of her suitors. The Scripture in Ephesians 6:2 was a law that had become a rule and was hanging over her head like a dead weight.

She came to me for advice, not wanting to disobey nor dishonour her parents. It was quite clear to me that a law had been turned into a rule without her knowing about it. She was being controlled by her mum who simply did not want to relinquish control to anyone else. I told her to obey her parents in the Lord, but outside of the Lord to disobey them with full honour.

A righteous stand looks like a rebellious stand, the difference is the attitude of the one making the stand to set the boundary. Had David not learnt this principle, he would never had been king. To disobey honourably takes skill and great fear of the

Lord. When most people find out that their pastors, parents or bosses are in violation of God's law, they disobey dishonourably. David ran from his spiritual father King Saul for years, but did it all with honour even though Saul was in the wrong. One time David had Saul dead to rights and could have killed him. Take a look at what happened.

> Abishai said to David, "Today God has delivered your enemy into your hands. Now let me pin him to the ground with one thrust of the spear; I won't strike him twice."
>
> But David said to Abishai, "Don't destroy him! Who can lay a hand on the Lord's anointed and be guiltless? As surely as the Lord lives," he said, "the Lord himself will strike him, or his time will come and he will die, or he will go into battle and perish.
>
> But the Lord forbid that I should lay a hand on the Lord's anointed. Now get the spear and water jug that are near his head, and let's go."
> 1 Samuel 26:8-11 (NIV)

Most people haven't yet learned to disobey dishonourably because they feel the two are mutually inclusive - that somehow you can't have one without the other and this is a lie. The truth is following God's law absolutely will always be perceived as rebellion by those who follow rules that they think are laws. Do it anyway.

Religious and political spirits
The spirits behind the cult of culture

The forces behind culture are not the same physical taskmasters of Egypt, but rather are spirits that whilst invisible, are all too felt in the world around us. Jesus actually warned us of this long ago, saying,

> *"Be careful," Jesus warned them. "Watch out for the yeast of the Pharisees and that of Herod."*
> *Mark 8:15 (NIV)*

Jesus's life and ministry were constantly harassed by these two spirits. The Pharisees represent the religious spirit, whilst King Herod represents the political spirit.

Yeast is a unicellular fungus culture that once placed in dough makes it rise. The enemy wants to insert the fungal infection of religion and politics into our everyday lives to keep us beholden to the cult of culture.

Much has been said by other authors about religious spirits. With the following definitions, I am attempting to provide insight into how these spirits operate and how to identify them.

1. The religious spirit

A religious spirit is a demonic spirit that forms the driving force behind a confused and deeply entrenched concept of God, even embracing false offences towards God. It can be identified in:

- **The religious mindset** habitually expresses fear based thoughts and behaviours that are deeply entrenched within a person's psychology informing them on how to see and interpret God and others around them.

- **A religious person** is driven by a confused and deeply entrenched concept of God!

- **A religious group** has an obsession with outdated truth, over an updated truth, that informs and conforms that group into an elite and exclusive cabal who's misguided zeal leads them to delusions of grandeur and a false responsibility that their mission is to convert others to their way of thinking, being, worshipping and doing. (sectarianism)

2. The political spirit

A political spirit is a demonic spirit that forms the driving force, incitement and the sense of offense behind the policing of words and the microaggression phenomenon. It can be identified in:

- **The Political Mindset** believes that people and philosophies can be divided beyond race and subject matter into sophisticated protected classes, subgroups and archetypes (stereotypes) warranting protection from subjective perceived verbal harm!

- **A political person** is an individual who adopts, as a duty, the policing of both their own and other people's words, not however to understand the true meaning of those words and their intent, but rather to investigate to whom said words can be potentially harmful or offensive! Once investigated the recourse is to censor said words or impose upon the speaker, through intimidation, the adoption of less harmful euphemisms.

- **A political group** is the opprobrious (negative) group think and mob like behaviour of an often small people group united by common victimhood. A collective of ideas, theories and philosophies converted by popular demand into facts without following or finding an actual fact pattern and the imposition of glaringly false facts upon the wider dissenting community in order to enforce conformity through mob justice, intimidation, censorship and irreparable online reputation damage.

When the two spirits collaborate

Through the early years of Jesus ministry, the spirit of religion operated in isolation to intimidate Jesus into conformity. Be careful of those who don't come to learn from you but instead come to test you.

> *Some Pharisees came to him to test him*
> *Matthew 19:3 (NIV)*

The internet, especially Facebook, is full of those who take it upon themselves to test every sentence you say, instead of embracing the whole truth, they focus on semantics and minutiae. They have no ability to track the issue, but rather they want to hone in on topics, so they can accuse you.

> *They were using this question as a trap, in order to have a*
> *basis for accusing Him.*
> *John 8:6 (NIV)*

The Pharisees were the thought leaders of their days and would gather to test Jesus' doctrine. Most of these called themselves 'experts in the law', but really were following rules as if they were laws . The Pharisees tried to intimidate Jesus into obscurity. However, the more they tried, the more viral Jesus's message went as every answer He gave either insulted them deeply or silenced them completely. You have to be as bold as a lion if you are going to survive this dark cosmopolitan age in which even those who claim to be on your side are the very ones trying to trip you up.

> *A man's enemies will be the members of his own*
> *household.*
> *Matthew 10:36 (NIV)*

Tough skin is a must for this emerging generation.

In the latter days of Jesus life, he noticed a collaboration of two spirits starting to form in which he called the 'yeast' of the religion and politics.

> *"Be careful," Jesus warned them. "Watch out for the yeast*
> *of the Pharisees and that of Herod."*
> *Mark 8:15 (NIV)*

There are commonalities behind the religious and political spirit, but also differences.

A RELIGIOUS SPIRIT	A POLITICAL SPIRIT
Moralises the immoral	Legalises the immoral
Makes the unthinkable, acceptable	Makes the acceptable, legal

A religious spirit promotes subjective, normative and obsessive behaviours (rules) through traditional enforcement i.e. through manipulation, fear, denominationalism, control, sectarianism.

A political spirit converts subjective, normative and obsessive behaviours into new legal instruments and policies to protect the religious spirit from voices of dissent.

Whilst both these spirits are concerned with words and behaviours, the religious spirit is concerned with conformity of words, speech and behaviour, whilst the political spirit is concerned with criminal or civil enforcement of the violation of words, speech and behaviours. The religious spirit will turn tradition into rules; the political spirit will turn rules into laws. In essence, the political spirit enforces what the religious spirit endorses.

Sadly, most religious spirits don't agree with political thoughts of the day, but in moments of expediency, the enemy of my enemy can quite easily become my friend when it can lead to the ending of a repugnant heresy that the religious spirit does not agree with. Through censorship and peer pressure, the religious spirit has forced the church into retreat mode and silence. A silence that has led to a form of endorsement I call endorsement by omission.

The power of euphemism

The key difference in how speech is moderated by a religious spirit and a political spirit is in the respective choice of euphemisms that both spirits create out of convenience as a hedging strategy against reprisal.

A religious spirit will put a euphemism on good words that it deems bad, whereas a political spirit will put a euphemism on bad words that it deems to be good.

> Woe to those who call evil good, and good evil; who substitute darkness for light and light for darkness; who substitute bitter for sweet and sweet for bitter!
> Isaiah 5:20 (CSB)

Instead of masturbation, pornography addiction and sexuality, the church has opted for the bulk term, 'the spirit of lust'. Instead of the word money, the church has opted for the term, 'blessing'. None of the original words are off limit words, even though some of the behaviours may be off limit behaviours, but they are deemed as worldly. Accordingly, the church by and large does not teach on these direct issues and, by neglecting to do so, delegates that duty to the world. As a result, our school teachers, who are not so sheepish, are empowered by government to indoctrinate (not educate) our children from as young as 7 in most cases to believe things that are demonstrably wrong.

In contrast, the political spirit will put a euphemism on words such as infanticide and instead of calling it infanticide opt for 'family planning, abortion, women's reproductive rights and 'the right to choose'. The power of the euphemism has been where the political spirit and religious spirit have succeeded in drastically shaping culture.

In swapping the labels, we make things that are unacceptable acceptable. Both a religious and political spirit team up to turn the exception into the rule by changing the question to suit the answer. This is by it is so common to hear that a matter is not about abortion, but is about a woman's rights to choose over her body; it is not about gay marriage, but about the right to love and marry whomsoever you want to marry and if you are against love, then you are full of hatred. It is argued that this is not about controlling speech (in that one day people, who teach truth will be one day penalised), but is rather about protecting people from 'hate speech' that may be detrimental to their mental health.

The 'this is not about…' argument has replaced reality and has put the church on a back foot. Eventually groups are formed in the interest of enforcing new rules and then turning those rules into laws so that mankind is forced to follow them and indeed tax fund them.

When the Pharisees met the Herodians
In the Gospels, we see the devil send these religious spirits to attack Jesus,

> *Then the Pharisees went out and plotted to trap Jesus in*
> *His words.*
> *Matthew 22:15 (NIV)*

However, right near the end of Jesus life, we see a slight plot twist. It is so subtle that if we gloss over the Bible we might have just missed it.

> *Later they sent some of the Pharisees and Herodians to*
> *Jesus to catch him in his words.*
> *Mark 12:13 (NIV)*

The religious spirit can control you, but it cannot kill you. Only when something religious becomes something political can there be death. The Pharisees plotted to kill Jesus, but they needed the Herodians to carry it out.

Today's speech trap

The partnering of the religious (Pharisees) with the political (Herodians) created a spiritual climate much like today. A PC (politically correct) culture is totally demonic. We see in Scripture, however, that an environment that would force lesser men into obscurity only seemed to embolden Jesus.

The time will come when, through active endorsement by the church or more fatally 'endorsement by omission', the world system will turn rules into laws unless the church lifts the gag order of religious silence and becomes a voice again. This merger of two spirits will bring great danger to the Western church. This is a speech trap, a snare of the enemy to one day deem the very Scriptures as hate speech! There will be those that will arise with more deliberate intent to monitor church services to catch pastors in their words. Political groups and activists will pretend to be honest Sunday goers to report church activity to authorities to impose fines, sanctions and even possible prison sentences upon them.

*Keeping a close watch on him, they sent spies, who
pretended to be sincere. They hoped to catch Jesus in
something he said, so that they might hand him over to the
power and authority of the governor.*
Luke 20:20

The Handover

*Then the Jewish leaders took Jesus from Caiaphas to the
palace of the Roman governor. By now it was early
morning, and to avoid ceremonial uncleanness they did not
enter the palace, because they wanted to be able to eat the
Passover. So Pilate came out to them and asked, "What
charges are you bringing against this man?"*

*"If he were not a criminal," they replied, "we would not have
handed him over to you."*

*Pilate said, "Take him yourselves and judge him by your
own law." "But we have no right to execute anyone," they
objected. This took place to fulfil what Jesus had said about
the kind of death he was going to die.*
John 18:28-32 (NIV)

The religious spirit has the power of intimidation, but the
political spirit has the power of execution. When the two come
together then they set a new precedent to shut down the
voices of God through the prophets and prophetic people. See
here in Scripture how the religious leaders handed Jesus over
to the government and even the government was confused.
Jesus had violated no laws, he merely violated religious
tradition. However, the rule following religious church

partnered with the government at a time of mutual expediency to conveniently do away with Jesus.

This is why prophets and prophetic people are so needed in today's age. The prophets are not opinion pieces; they are mouth pieces of God. Religious spirits will naturally hate them and will hand them over to be killed, because they break all the religious rules.

> *"I also raised up prophets from among your children and Nazirites from among your youths. Is this not true, people of Israel?" declares the Lord. "But you made the Nazirites drink wine and commanded the prophets not to prophesy. Amos 2:11-12*

The protection of words is the protection of spirits and, ultimately, the protection of culture. If you don't speak truth, but speak subject to the religious and political atmosphere, then you further entrench a spirits' survival in the church and world.

> *For the time will come when people will not put up with sound doctrine. Instead, to suit their own desires, they will gather around them a great number of teachers to say what their itching ears want to hear.*
> *2 Timothy 4:3 (NIV)*

> *Who say to the seers, "You must not see visions"; And to the prophets, "You must not prophesy to us what is right, Speak to us pleasant words, Prophesy illusions.*
> *Isaiah 30:10(NASB)*

Two different spirits requiring two different approaches

So just how do you deal with those in your work place, church or government who want to hand you over to the political spirit to face the consequence of being fired, censored publicly shamed or even imprisoned and killed?

> *Waiting to catch Him in something He might say.*
> *Luke 11:54*

When Jesus dealt with the religious spirit, he often always dealt with it by offending them directly or doing the very thing they told Him He could not do. Why? Because that's all they are, rules!

> *Then the disciples came to him and asked, "Do you know*
> *that the Pharisees were offended when they heard this?"*
> *Matthew 15:12*

Never, and I repeat, never surrender to the religious spirit. It may hate you online, show up at all your meetings, tweet about you or pressure you to stay part of a body you no longer agree with, but you must never surrender to a religious spirit. Following its rules is akin to perpetuating an environment that will eventually become a breeding ground for a political spirit to step into.

Remember, rules are not laws and whilst laws are penalised judicially, the violation of rules is only enforced by peer pressure. You are under no obligation to follow rules. However, when the religious spirit recognises that it is failing, then it will partner with an equally suspicious political spirit to scan your words for legal violations or workplace infringements. Notice how Jesus dealt with a political and religious spirit.

> At this, the leaders sought to arrest Jesus, for they knew that He had spoken this parable against them. But fearing the crowd, they left Him and went away. Later, they sent some of the Pharisees and Herodians to catch Jesus in His words.
>
> "Teacher," they said, "we know that You are honest and are swayed by no one. Indeed, You are impartial and teach the way of God in accordance with the truth. Now then, is it lawful to pay taxes to Caesar or not? Should we pay them or not?"
>
> But Jesus saw through their hypocrisy and said, "Why are you testing Me? Bring Me a denarius to inspect."
>
> So they brought it, and He asked them, "Whose likeness is this? And whose inscription?" "Caesar's," they answered.
>
> Then Jesus told them, "Give to Caesar what is Caesar's, and to God what is God's."
> And they marvelled at Him....
> Mark 12:12-16

Jesus taught what I call a 'creative gospel'. Parables were stealth gospels intended to sniper out religious and political spirits without altering the truth. With religion, Jesus was very blunt and impatient, but when politics and religion combined, Jesus was very political, wise, yet still just as bold. I like to think that He learnt this likely from John's mistake of dealing with both spirits the same way!

But when John saw many of the Pharisees and Sadducees
coming to his place of baptism, he said to them, "You brood
of vipers, who warned you to flee from the coming wrath?
And many other things in his exhortation preached he unto
the people. But Herod the tetrarch, being reproved by him
for Herodias his brother Philip's wife, and for all the evils
which Herod had done, Added yet this above all, that he
shut up John in prison.
Luke 3:18-20

It's just bad for business when religion and politics combine in
your workplace, ministry or business. John lost his head for
trying to deal with the political spirit the same way he dealt with
a religious spirit.
Whereas religious spirits have no power of execution, political
spirits do! Therefore, in order to savour your time on earth, it
helps to be wise as serpents and meek as lambs.

In conclusion, to break free from the cult of culture and to
ultimately transform it, you and I must be willing to find rules
worth breaking and then break them!

Don't become so well-adjusted to your culture that you fit
into it without even thinking. Instead, fix your attention on
God. You'll be changed from the inside out. Readily
recognise what he wants from you, and quickly respond to
it. Unlike the culture around you, always dragging you down
to its level of immaturity, God brings the best out of you,
develops well-formed maturity in you.
Romans 12:2 [The Message]

Chapter Eight

Understanding Heaven's Political Constitution

The Polis, the Agora and the Ekklesia

Christianity is not a religion, it is a government.

For to us a child is born, to us a son is given, and the government will be on his shoulders.
Isaiah 9:6

It is important to understand the constitution of this government so that we can know our rights, duties and operations within it.

According to Merriam Webster, a constitution is:

the structure, composition, physical makeup, or nature of something

The Book of Hebrews 12 is a Book of our constitution.

For you have not come to the mountain that may be touched and that burned with fire, and to blackness and darkness and tempest, and the sound of a trumpet and the voice of words, so that those who heard it begged that the word should not be spoken to them anymore. (For they could not endure what was commanded: "And if so much as a beast touches the mountain, it shall be stoned or shot with an arrow." And so terrifying was the sight that Moses said, "I am exceedingly afraid and trembling.") But you

have come to Mount Zion and to the city of the living God,
the heavenly Jerusalem, to an innumerable company of
angels, to the general assembly and church of the firstborn
who are registered in heaven, to God the Judge of all, to
the spirits of just men made perfect, to Jesus the Mediator
of the new covenant, and to the blood of sprinkling that
speaks better things than that of Abel.
Hebrews 12:18-24

In this chapter, we find the anatomy or make up of the
Kingdom of God. Let me list this for you.

1. The Polis (City) of the Living God
2. The Angels
3. The Agora (General Assembly)
4. The Ekklessia (Church)
5. God the Judge
6. Jesus the mediator

These six institutions make up the sum total of God's
distribution of powers and each one serves a vital role in the
make up or constitution of the Kingdom of Heaven and its
distribution of powers.

Each order plays a significant role; some more so in Heaven
than on Earth and others more so in Earth than in Heaven.
However, it helps to understand that this is not a strict code.
For instance, the angels operate in Heaven and in Earth. (See
Genesis 28:12, John 1:51)

Jesus has finished momentarily His earthly role and now
presides in heaven. His role in the Earth has at least for the

mean time been fulfilled. (See Psalm 110:1, Matthew 22:44, Acts 3:20). Jesus' occupation is now totally administrative; He is the mediator of the peace treaty brokered between God and man that satisfies the judgement of God that was against us and He serves as a reminder to God of a promise He made to one day redeem us even though we are in the flesh.

God is the Judge and, as chief magistrate of the Supreme Court, His duty is to:

1. Hear our case (Isaiah 43:26, Jeremiah 12:1)
2. Judge fairly in the administration of all mankind (Matthew 5:45, Psalm 89:14)
3. Oversee the proceedings of the Ekklesia and affirm or veto requests that are not established precedents in heaven. (Matthew 16:19)
4. Listen to the cases presented by the chief prosecution and Attorney General of World (Lucifer) and hear his case against the saints, plus supporting arguments from the defendant (Holy Spirit) against the prosecution as uttered through the Ekklesia. (Revelation 12:10, Job 1)
5. Oversee the distribution of angels as executioners of the Word of God. (Matthew 26:53)

Now let us talk about the more earthly bodies that play a significant role in the administration of the earth.

The Polis

> *But you have come to Mount Zion and to the city of the living God, the heavenly Jerusalem*
> *Hebrews 12:22*

The word *'City'* is the Greek word Polis. The Bible says that we are called to the Polis of the living God. The word *'city'* is where we get the word 'citizen' from. I believe this is important because for so long we have been defined as a church and not as a citizen. The church is not the citizenry, the church is the embassy responsible for how the citizenry advances the practices and exercises the rights of its country in a foreign country. We will talk about this in greater detail later on.

Jesus was invested in letting us know who we were from the onset. He made the same claim as Apostle Paul did in Hebrews 12:22

> *"You are the light of the world. A city set on a hill cannot be hidden;*
> *Matthew 5:14*

You are a City on a hill that cannot be hidden! That hill or mountain is called Zion. Established above every other mountain

Beacons

In the previous chapter, we spoke about how the prophetic being called to *'phos phemi'* - to give light or reveal. In this chapter, I want to help you understand how that light should be administered to make the Body of Christ the beacon of hope for the nations as God intended her to be.

This light is delivered and administered through the Polis. The Polis was the administrative and religious City Centre of

Greece. This political entity was ruled by a body of peoples (citizens) known as the '*ekklesia*'.

The polis gave rise to derivative terms that we use in our common English today. Terms like:

1. Policy - A government statement of intent
2. Politics - The art or science of governance
3. Polity - A form or process of civil government or constitution
4. Police - Law enforcement

It is safe to say, where there is no polis (representative government of the Kingdom of Heaven) in a nation, there are:

1. Bad policies
2. Bad politics
3. Bad polity
4. Bad policing

Every saint is a member or CITIzen of the CITy known as Zion and must know this so that representative government is not solely vested in special church leaders. Saints are policy makers. In every area of society they are meant to be politically inclined to partner with Heaven to release God's statement of intent into the earth so that the Earth's political philosophy might come into in alignment with the political philosophy of Heaven.

But, just what are God's policies?

Discovering Heaven's political philosophy

1. Righteousness and Justice

Righteousness and justice are the foundation of your throne; love and faithfulness go before you.
Psalm 89:14

The most consequential part of God's political philosophy is righteousness and justice. This is not just an idea of God or an option. This is what makes His throne an everlasting throne. If God were to change these two philosophies, then His throne would be corrupted much like the thrones of the earth.

Righteousness means a moral right! In God, there is no such thing as moral relativity. Moral relativism heralds a notion that morality can be based on a particular standpoint and that something can be morally right for one person and morally wrong for another. Righteousness is an absolute standpoint on morality, that all actions are either right or wrong.

The subjectivity of morality in our world today has even redefined God's view of equity and equality. By using the same words but slightly and cunningly changing their meaning, Satan has moved many in the church into what I call 'perverted justice'.

The 'Black Lives Matter' movement was started in 2013 after the death of Trayvon Martin and the acquittal of his killer George Zimmerman. In 2020, Black Lives Matter saw a dramatic resurgence in popularity following the fatal death of George Floyd. The fight was a noble one, justice for black lives, especially those who were killed at the hands of white police officers. It was easy to see the appeal and many churches in the African-American community joined forces to solidify this growing movement. 'No justice No peace' echoed around the world as a once small organisation swelled into a social justice behemoth.

Surely God would be on the side of such an efficacious movement. I believe what started the BLM movement was the abdication of the church towards God's policy of justice and, in particular, the plight of African-Americans. In our pursuit of a more righteous world where people are led to Jesus, the only one who can produce righteousness, we resigned the world to pursue justice among pseudo-leftist reverends and extremist groups who pursued justice but forsook righteousness.

Righteousness void of justice metastasises into vengeance and dominance. Righteousness and justice are one word to God. One simply cannot exist without the other. In the world's pursuit of justice, they abdicated righteousness. Justice that isn't right, is wrong, no matter what outcome it produces to favour the one seeking it.

2. Nations and Boundaries

Our God has always been a God of nations and boundaries. God is not a globalist! He loves national identity and national patriotism. Neither is God an isolationist. God is not looking for hermit kingdoms, neither is he looking for dependent ones, but interdependent nations.

Globalism and globalisation are two evils because, in order for them to succeed, a political philosophy needs to deal with any defectors from the structure. These philosophies known as socialism and communism, have always turned benevolent dictators, oligarchs and plutocrats into draconian and Orwellian leaders.

Globalism only works when everybody's political philosophy favours one another. The first man to try out this experiment long before the elites like George Soros and Klaus Schwab (World Economic Forum founder) was a man named Nimrod.

> *Now the whole world had one language and a common speech. As people moved eastward, they found a plain in Shinar[b] and settled there. They said to each other, "Come, let's make bricks and bake them thoroughly." They used brick instead of stone, and tar for mortar. Then they said, "Come, let us build ourselves a city, with a tower that reaches to the heavens, so that we may make a name for ourselves; otherwise we will be scattered over the face of the whole earth."But the Lord came down to see the city and the tower the people were building. The Lord said, "If as one people speaking the same language they have begun to do this, then nothing they plan to do will be impossible for them. Come, let us go down and confuse their language so they will not understand each other." So the Lord scattered them from there over all the earth, and they stopped building the city.*
> *Genesis 11:1-8*

God came down to see the City (Policies) that men were building. God does not celebrate the policy of globalism, nor will He ever, because it is built on humanism and secularism. To date mankind whether through multinationals or federations have been trying to rebuild this policy and have failed up until recently. What changed? I believe in Genesis, God confused their language, in doing so they had no common way to communicate. Cultures were created and tribes and each one more complex than the last.

When Babel was built the second time under Nebuchadnezzar, He began to teach again but notice this time, he did not teach the language alone, he needed to teach both language and literature of Babylon.

> *young men in whom there was no blemish, but good-looking, gifted in all wisdom, possessing knowledge and quick to understand, who had ability to serve in the king's palace, and whom they might teach the language and literature of the Chaldeans.*
> *Daniel 1:4*

The secret to understanding what is going on now is to look at what our young people are being taught in universities and colleges today. Our languages may be different but all over the world our literature is becoming the same. Majority of today's young people view capitalism as evil and Marxism as good. Majority of today's young people despise their parents' way as old fashioned and a lot of them have thrown out the celebration of the nuclear family and patriarchal society as outdated. Suspending with God's way is the largest plan of globalism to undo the name of God and His anointed Son Jesus. It is to denigrate the nuclear family and in doing so create a government paternal surrogate.

David saw this same phenomenon trying to play itself out in his day when he said.

*Why do the nations rage and the peoples plot in vain? The
kings of the earth rise up and the rulers band together
against the LORD and against his anointed
Psalm 2:1-2*

Globalism sounds prima-facie like an excellent strive towards a
more progressive and inclusive society, but it only succeeds if
it rules out 'religion' as what it deems a huge hinderance in its
success. Globalism only succeeds where there are no free
thinkers, where personal opinion is strongly discouraged,
speech and even thought is carefully policed and where
anyone that does not align to secular orthodox is censored,
voices of descent are cancelled or worse off killed.

3. Capitalism Versus Socialism

God's government empowers; Satan's government enables.
God's government devolves whilst Satan's government
consolidates. God favours small government that gives as
much power to His people as possible. The smaller the
government, the less likely the chance for dictatorial or
draconian leadership. God gives power to the five-fold, whose
job it is to give power to the saints (See Ephesians 4)

God does not like government that lords over, but rather
government that serves in the empowerment of the people.

*Jesus said to them, "The kings of the Gentiles lord it over
them; and those who exercise authority over them call
themselves Benefactors. But you are not to be like that.
Instead, the greatest among you should be like the
youngest, and the one who rules like the one who serves.*

The people are the benefactors of good governance not the government. When any government benefits more from its governance than the people do, then that is bad and failing government. When government gets too big it oversteps its boundaries. Instead of being a benefactor of the people, it benefits from the people by installing policies that favour racketeering, pay for play, quantitative easing and tax schemes designed deliberately to enrich the government by stealing its wealth from its own people. Whilst social structures exist in Heaven, God is very much a feudal capitalist. We see this throughout Scripture. One such instance is His deliverance of the children of Israel from socialist Egypt. Moreover, we see this intent play itself out in the parable of the talents. (See Matthew 25:14)

God's fiscal philosophy ends with this:

> *So take the bag of gold from him and give it to the one who*
> *has ten bags. For whoever has will be given more, and they*
> *will have an abundance. Whoever does not have, even*
> *what they have will be taken from them.*
> *Matthew 25:28-29*

Isn't this interesting that God does not give the bags of gold to the one who had the second most or even the one who had the least, he gave it to the one who had the most. In my book (Kingdom Secrets Jesus Couldn't Share... Until Now), I talk about this in much greater detail. It is important to understand, God's political philosophy favours capitalism, but not the crony and corrupt capitalism of today that is incestuously married to government and lobbying interests to monopolise the market and build unnatural organisations, but rather a free market philosophy, one that leaves the market to correct itself by competing against bad products and good products. We are yet to see a leader brave enough to end the lobbying for policies of the right wing and the attack on free market employment by left wing unions. A truly successful government is one that empowers its people instead of enabling them.

God did give Israel government bread for a season. He fed them on manna, not that they might be dependent on it but rather that He might slowly wean them off from the government subsidies they were used to and the food stamps of Egypt back to dependency on God for daily bread.

> He humbled you, causing you to hunger and then feeding you with manna, which neither you nor your ancestors had known, to teach you that man does not live on bread alone but on every word that comes from the mouth of the LORD.
> Deuteronomy 8:3

These are just a few key points on Heaven's political philosophy and it was wise men that were meant to teach it to us so that we can partner with redeemable qualities of kings in the earth. These wise men were known as apostles/sages, prophets and teachers.

> Therefore I am sending you prophets and sages and teachers. Some of them you will kill and crucify; others you will flog in your synagogues and pursue from town to town.
> Matthew 23:34

The Agora

We are called to the general assembly. The word here *panéguris*, it is broken into two words pas meaning all, *agora* meaning marketplace. One of my favourite definitions of marketplace is taken from Websters dictionary. It reads:

"A sphere in which intangible values compete for acceptance".

We are all called to the marketplace whether we like it or not. It is in the marketplace that our intangible values or policies compete for acceptance among a barrage of other ideologies and world religions. Christianity today by and large has sanitised God from what they define as the mainstream. Remember, God is the Mainstream! Everything flows from Him and it is He that desires to reconcile all things back to Him.

We do not need to sanitise God from a world that He put us in the Earth to affect. Throughout Scripture we see that this Gospel is not supposed to be in our mouths solely, but much more in our feet.

How beautiful on the mountains are the feet of those who bring good news, who proclaim peace, who bring good

tidings, who proclaim salvation, who say to Zion, "Your God reigns!"
Isaiah 52:7

Our job is to proclaim to the Agora that our God reigns over every sphere of the Earth. Apostle Paul admonishes Ephesus to have their feet shod with the readiness of the gospel of peace. (See Ephesians 6:15)

If we are being told to put our gospel shoes on, just where are we going. We are going to the Agora. We must be ready there to compete among a plethora of religions, industries, ideologies, economic philosophies and to establish in each one, the rulership of our God through the exercise of the mind of Christ.

We have the mind of Christ
1 Corinthians

Many Christians don't know the mind of Christ on the marketplace. Some often treat political/social and economic illiteracy as if it were a virtue. That somehow it is the churches job to cast these aside as fleeting carnalities. In our bid to sanitise God from the secular deluge, instead of going into the agora, we 'agorise' the church. We build archives in which we compete for acceptance among ourselves. We create award shows for ourselves, genres of music that we can sit comfortably in, TV channels that we can compete among ourselves for airtime in and whilst there is little wrong with this, it creates this delusion of our own grandeur. Our measurement is no longer how many people in the world has my music impacted with the rulership of Christ, but rather how has it sold among my Christian fan base. To be effective in the agora, we need market penetration not church/market integration. This was Jesus concern when He came into the temple.

> To those who sold doves he said, "Get these out of here! Stop turning my Father's house into a market!"
> John 2:16

Instead of competing in the market, the church of Jesus' day had found a way to integrate the market into the church and measure their success by content only their echo chamber would be satisfied to watch, view, buy or listen to. Does that sound an awful lot like our modern church? Instead of competing for acceptance in the world and creating content that rivals the ideas of Darwin, Dawkins and the thought leaders of our world today, we opt for competing among our own genres. I must stress, there is nothing wrong with this, but I believe prophetically that God is taking us from church/market integration into market penetration

According to Investopedia, market penetration relates to the number of potential customers that have purchased a specific company's product instead of a competitor's product. To succeed in the agora, you must be willing to let both grow together!

> Jesus told them another parable: "The kingdom of heaven is like a man who sowed good seed in his field. But while everyone was sleeping, his enemy came and sowed weeds among the wheat, and went away. When the wheat sprouted and formed heads, then the weeds also

appeared. "The owner's servants came to him and said, 'Sir, didn't you sow good seed in your field? Where then did the weeds come from?' "'An enemy did this,' he replied. "The servants asked him, 'Do you want us to go and pull them up?'

"'No,' he answered, 'because while you are pulling the weeds, you may uproot the wheat with them. **Let both grow together** *until the harvest. At that time I will tell the harvesters: First collect the weeds and tie them in bundles to be burned; then gather the wheat and bring it into my barn.*
Matthew 13:24-29

In the agora, God is not supposed to be sanitized out, but rather both the wheat and the weeds are supposed to compete for market penetration.

We are in the midst of a clashing of the swords, where finally what has felt like a slow-motion reel of the church to the agora is finally getting to release an almighty seismic clash and in the midst of it the church is going to get a revelation - that light is far more powerful, consequential and potent than darkness.

The agora functioned in Ancient Greece as a political and commercial space. From agora came the two Greek verbs ἀγοράζω, agorázō, "I shop", and ἀγορεύω, agoreúō, "I speak." Not only is the church supposed to be mercantile, but we are supposed to gather to the political square to voice our Kingdom policies. This was the common practice of Jesus.

And wherever he went--into villages, towns or countryside-- they placed the sick in the marketplaces *(Agora). They*

begged him to let them touch even the edge of his cloak,
and all who touched it were healed.
Mark 6:56

Jesus knew that the agora was the place where intellectuals, religious leaders, political figures, entertainers and mystics gathered, so he positioned His light in the same marketplaces and was willing to compete among a wide range of powers all vying for the same public acceptance and market penetration. He wanted to release the mainstream and do it with such excellence that people had no choice but to opt for His far more superior power and demonstration.

Apostle Paul would reason with the Greek philosophers because he understood their political philosophy could alter the face of civilised society. In order to do so, he would have had to have been well cultured and well read. He met in their agora often.

So he reasoned in the synagogue with both Jews and God-fearing Greeks, as well as in the marketplace day by day with those who happened to be there
Acts 17:17

Agoraphobia means the fear of open spaces. The term denotes a phobic condition in which the sufferer becomes anxious in environments that are unfamiliar – for instance, places where they perceive that they have little control. Such anxiety may be triggered by wide-open spaces, by crowds, or by some public situations, and the psychological term derives from the agora as a large and open gathering place.

My prayer for you is that God delivers you from the agoraphobia that has been limiting you from market penetration.

The interface through which the world relates with the church is called Babylon. It is a system based on a political philosophy that is opposed to the philosophy of the Kingdom of Heaven. When Daniel penetrated this interface, he had to learn the things that the interface was requiring so he could pass through and be effective and unnoticed. This is from where the term Cosmopolitan Christian is coined. Daniel would have had to have learnt to become a Cosmopolite without compromise.

> Then the king ordered Ashpenaz, the chief of his court officials, to bring in some Israelites from the royal family and the nobility—young men without blemish, handsome, gifted in all wisdom, knowledgeable, quick to understand, and qualified to serve in the king's palace—and to teach them the language and literature of the Chaldeans
> Daniel 1:3-4

Note the requirements were
1. Youth
2. No physical defects
3. Good looking
4. Studious
5. Qualifications

Babylon wants fresh blood. It is extremely judgmental and cares more about packaging than content. Although content is important, youthful good looks go a long way in securing your place in Babylon. This is why, when one watches a program like the music talent show, X Factor, Simon Cowell is quick to point out the attractive qualities of the talent, often stating that singing can be worked out later. All major industries of the world want to know that you are qualified so it helps to stay in school even if you don't plan on using your degree, a qualification goes a long way in passing through Babylon's radar.

In order to affect Babylon or the agora, one must be willing to engage in this 'beauty pageant' of sorts. Like Queen Esther, you must understand what the interface wants and concede to the standards of excellence without being compromised by the decadence of the system.

You must decide like Daniel not to defile yourself with the systems choice meals. (Daniel 1:8)

Somebody will say, this sounds like a lot of work! Transforming the world is apostolic not pastoral! You must be willing to become all things to all men and put on the disguises like serpents, but have gentleness like doves.

> *"I'm sending you out like sheep among wolves. So be as cunning as snakes but as innocent as doves.*
> *Matthew 10:16*

The 'sending out' is the word *apostellō*. Every saint is apostolic not pastoral. Pastoral saints tend to favour safety and sanctuary over risk and reward. An apostolic mission is military grade, top level security clearance, special ops. It requires the believer to deploy tactical skills including stealth and the prudence to get on the other side of the enemy lines. Pastoral saints usually wait for the battles to come to them, Apostolic ones are sent directly on a mission behind enemy lines.

To be cunning means that you become wise. Jesus was pointing to the stealth of satan when he made this very point. In Genesis 3:1 the serpent was defined as more cunning than any other beast of the field that the Lord God had made.

Synonyms include:
> Wise - aware of or informed about a particular matter, intelligent
>
> Crafty - adept in the use of subtlety and cunning
>
> Prudent - marked by wisdom or judiciousness
>
> Subtle - Delicate and elusive

These tactical weapons of sagacity and intelligence are the kind of skills needed to enter into work for the United States CIA or FBI. When the FBI go under cover, they have what is known as a handler. The handler is the person on the other side that the inside operative reports to in an undisclosed location. The undercover agent is known as the asset. The asset ceases to be an asset when

1. The asset's cover is compromised.
2. The asset has compromised - a term known as going rogue.

This is why Jesus demands us to be sagacious, but innocent and unwavering in our conviction. To compromise without being compromised is a hard line to tow.

Many of my friends who have gone into Hollywood with the intention to transform it have themselves been conformed to it. These have no handler. Esther's handler was Mordecai. Mordecai served as a reminder to Esther of her reason for winning the beauty pageant and being chosen in this original screening of 'The Bachelor'. Your handler is your Apostolic father. Their job is to pray for you and to hold you accountable to the mirror of God's word so that Babylon doesn't take you.

Remember Satan is cosmetic, so it is no wonder that he is on the hunt for attractive people. His beauty standards are high and superficial. May we prepare like Esther so we remain supernatural in a superficial world.

The Ekklesia

The Ekklessia is the embassy of God. It possesses or should posses:

Revelation
Apostles and Prophets
An equipping Centre
A house of Ambassadorial ministers

What is an Ekklesia?

A *kirke* or *'church'* which derives from the Latin word for 'Belonging to the Lord' is a translation from the King James Bible of what was originally called an *ekklesia*. Since being called the church, we have somewhat lost our original purpose as the ekklesia.

Ekklesia has a double barrel meaning.

Ek meaning 'out from or to' and *kaleo* meaning 'to call'. The Ekklesia was the rallying call for the Polis (citizens of the Kingdom of God) to gather to discuss, legislate, set foreign affair agendas, vote and hold judicial proceedings.

The Ekklesia is called out from the cosmetic and superficial world but also called to the cosmetic and superficial world from a foreign policy standpoint.

The Ekklesia is entirely enthralled in foreign policy. It is the mission of the Ekklesia to impact any world it is set up in with the policies of the Kingdom of heaven.

1. Revelation

Revelation is what separates ekklesia from *kirke*. Without a revelation there really is no reason for people to gather. Those assigned to assemble, assemble not because you serve tea's and coffee's but rather because revelation has forced them out of hiding.

Take for instance, RIG Nation. A mission founded on the revelation that God wants to restore Apostles and Prophets that will equip the saints for the work of ministry. Today 100,000 people have subscribed to become a part of that ekklesia. They did not gather around Tomi Arayomi; rather, they gathered around a revelation, a mystery that resonated with what they were carrying all along but had no language for.

Go and learn the meaning of this statement, *"There is no mystery in fellowship but there is fellowship in mystery."*

> *and to make all see what is the fellowship of the mystery, which from the beginning of the ages has been hidden in God who created all things through Jesus Christ;*
> *Ephesians 3:9*

The beauty of serving God is that when you understand the mystery God has put in you to steward, an ekklesia will rally around it. Some call this 'their tribe', this tribe carries your DNA and are central to the fulfilment of the mission as they each are a lively stone that together with your stone build up the spiritual house. (1 Peter 2:5)

2. Apostles and Prophets

> *Because of this, God in his wisdom said, 'I will send them*
> *prophets and apostles, some of whom they will kill and*
> *others they will persecute.'*
> *Luke 11:49*

Religion loves to kill the Apostles and Prophets. This doctrine of cessation has existed since the beginning of time (Luke 11:50). Apostles and Prophets are seasonal not 'sermonal'. Without them, churches have congregants instead of combatants. The key difference between the Apostle and the Prophet is the Apostle carries the revelation of the word, the Prophet carries the revelation of the future. When these revelatory titans combine, they release a hybridity in the saints that is truly more unique than a human bio-weapon.

The Apostle and the Prophet are both builder anointings. (See Jeremiah 1:10, 1 Corinthians 3:10). The emphasis lies however with the Apostle to build and the Prophet to see.

> *Unless the LORD builds the house, the builders labor in*
> *vain. Unless the LORD watches over the city, the guards*
> *stand watch in vain.*
> *Psalm 127:1*

Without the Apostle and the Prophet, the ekklesia becomes a Sunday church and a fertile ground for tradition, religious control and denominational introspection. What I mean by this is, they become inward focused, favouring the churches vision over the vision for the church in the region, nation and land. Prophets release the prophecy of Heaven, Apostles turn this prophecy into policy.

The order is and will always be in the ekklesia, first Apostles then Prophets.

> *And God has placed in the church first of all apostles,*
> *second prophets*
> *1 Corinthians 12:28*

3. An equipping Centre

The Apostle and the Prophet are chief equippers. An ekklesia is separated from a typical church when it is equipping focused and not enabling focused.

Enabling focused is a model built around the centricity of the pastor and pastoral team as the source of solution and aid. Equipping focused builds around the centricity of the saint and discovering their ministry with the Apostolic and Prophetic mission as the focus.

Enabling Focused	Equipping Focused
The leader Need to be Needed	The leader Leads to no longer be needed
Works themselves into more jobs	Works themselves out of a job
How can you help build my vision	How can I help build your part in our mutual vision
Your Value to me	My value to you
My Church	Christ's Church
Ownership Mentality	Stewardship Mentality

Enabling Focused	Equipping Focused
Withholding	Sending
Sanctuary Focus	School Focus
Saved to be safe	Saved to be sent

The church focus is for Christ through the saints to fill the sanctuary, the ekklesia focus is for Christ through the saints to fill all things.

> He who descended is also the One who ascended far
> above all the heavens, that He might fill all things.)
> Ephesians 4:10

4. A house of ambassadorial ministers

An ambassador is an accredited diplomat sent by a state as its permanent representative in a foreign Country. Our ministerial duty as the saints is diplomatic representation of our King in the earth. In order to achieve this, the ekklesia needs to be more foreign policy focused than it is domestic policy focused.

Foreign policy is the policy of a sovereign state in its interaction with other sovereign states. As representatives of the state, we must first recognise our political philosophy and how that policy can impact foreign nations and reconcile those nations back to the Lord.

> The seventh angel sounded his trumpet, and there were
> loud voices in heaven, which said: "The kingdom of the
> world has become the kingdom of our Lord and of his

Messiah, and he will reign for ever and ever."
Revelation 11:15

There are several power structures and each one complex in its nature. Understanding these power structures is key to defining nations redemptive qualities.

Below is a list of 5 main power structures in our world today:

1. **Anarchy** - *a society without a publicly enforced government or political authority. A situation where there is no state.*
2. **Confederation** – *a union of sovereign states*
3. **Federation** – *a union of partially self-governing states under a central federal government.*
4. **Unitary State** – *where central government is ultimately supreme. Any administrative divisions exercise only the powers the central govt chooses to delegate. Most States have this!*
5. **Kingdom** - *a realm ruled by a king.*

Our power structure is a Kingdom. Not so different from the Kingdoms of the Earth, except our King serves and has his functions administered through His Son, who has His functions administered through the church (or ekklesia).

These power structures each have different forms of administering their power. Below are the different forms of government.

1. **Autocracy** - *Supreme power concentrated in the hands of one person or polity, whose decisions are subject to neither external legal restraints nor*

regularised mechanisms of popular control. (Saudi Emirates, Soviet Union, Brunei, Oman)

2. **Democracy** - *Citizens exercise direct power or elect representatives among themselves to form a governing body such as a parliament.*
3. **Oligarchy** - *Rule of the few, power rests in a small number of people with distinguished wealth, family ties, education or military control. Often controlled by rich families who pass their control by inheritance from generation to generation.*
4. **Kritarchy** - *rule by various judges*
5. **Technocracy** - *Ruled by those with technical and scientific knowledge*
6. **Bureaucracy** - *Ruled by the state, as opposed to elected officials.*
7. **Stratocracy** - *A rule by military service, a system of government composed of military government in which the state and military are constitutionally the same thing.*

For a long time the Israel was ruled as a Kritachy. This Kritarchy, mostly made up of Prophets who became judges, was a suitable model for a transitory period in Israels history and formed the predicate upon which the Book of Judges was written. In the New Testament, God has transitioned into an Eklessia model.

According to Wikipedia,

> *The ecclesia or ekklesia (Greek: ἐκκλησία) was the principal assembly of the democracy of ancient Athens. It was the popular assembly, open to all male citizens as soon as they qualified for citizenship.[1] In 594 BC, Solon allowed all Athenian citizens to participate, regardless of*

class, even the thetes.[citation needed] The assembly was
responsible for declaring war, military strategy and electing
the strategoi and other officials.

Strategos or strategus, plural strategoi, (Greek:
στρατηγός, pl. στρατηγοί; Doric Greek: στραταγός,
stratagos; meaning "army leader") is used in Greek to
mean military general. In the Hellenistic world and the
Byzantine Empire the term was also used to describe a
military governor. In the modern Hellenic Army it is the
highest officer rank.

The New Testament church are congregants, the New
Testament eklessia are combatants. This military/diplomatic
hybrid is not common, as in most countries, those who wish to
enter into diplomatic or public service must relinquish their
military status, but the *strategos* ambassador must be willing to
engage both in diplomacy and if need be in combat.

God's Kingdom in the New Testament is not just a monarchy
but in Christ the constitution has evolved into a stratocracy. A
rule by military service, a system of government composed of
military government in which the State and military are
constitutionally the same thing.

The Spartan City State is a social system and constitution that
was completely focused on military training and excellence.
Honour orientated timocracy (a rule by the honourable).
Individuals of outstanding character or faculty are placed in the
seat of power.

This is why Apostle Paul said:

For the weapons of our warfare are not carnal but mighty in
God for pulling down strongholds,
2 Corinthians 10:4

The word warfare in the Greek is *strateia* and it means military campaign, expedition. Apostle Paul was speaking as a *stratocrat*. This word is where we in our English language derive the word strategy from.

God has put us in the Earth to strategise the formation of His Kingdom and political philosophy in the Earth as it is in heaven and we cannot succeed in our aims without the Apostolic and Prophetic ministry. Without the Apostle and the Prophet the church becomes service orientated and not strategy orientated. Our focus becomes the Sunday and not the everyday devising of God's agenda in the Earth and our capacity to strategise its fulfilment. We become soul orientated and not system orientated and to this end we win souls but they go back into many of the systems and philosophies of the world. Satan is system orientated, he sets up schemes (systemic agendas) to seed his agenda in the earth. So when God says go into all the world and preach the Gospel to all creation (Mark 16:15), we often miss the fact that there are three commissions. The Great Commission never mitigates the first two.

1. *Commission 1 - Have dominion (Genesis 1:26)*
2. *Commission 2 - Preach the Gospel of Good News (Mark 16:15)*
3. *Commission 3 - Make disciples of nations (Matthew 28:19)*

Disciple nations needs a foreign policy focus. God gives to every man and woman,

1. *A mission*
2. *A submission*

In Genesis 1, God defines the mission as dominion. In Genesis 2, God defines the sub-mission as domestic. God gives the man a family in Genesis 2, but a ministry in Genesis 1.

In Ephesians 5:21-31 & 6:1-9, Apostle Paul defines the sub-mission.

1. *Submit to one another out of reverence to Christ*
2. *Wives submit to and respect your husbands as to the Lord*
3. *Husbands love your wives as Christ loved the church*
4. *Children obey your parents in the Lord*
5. *Honour your Father and Mother*
6. *Fathers don't provoke your children to wrath*
7. *Employees obey and respect your employers*

All of this is not the mission. Remember, this is the domestic policy of heaven. Our ministry as ambassadors is foreign policy.

In verse 10, Paul lays out the foreign policy with this exhaling declaration,

Finally, my brethren...
Ephesians 6:10

182

It is as if Apostle Paul is sighing in relief. From verse 10 onwards, Paul goes from the sub-mission to the mission. Have we made a mission out of the submission? Are we guilty of using our churches as grounds to get the submission in order that we have not lived out the reason God installed the church in the first place.

> His intent was that now, through the church, the manifold wisdom of God should be made known to the rulers and authorities in the heavenly realms,
> Ephesians 3:10

Paul makes this statement, *we wrestle not against flesh and blood but against principalities and powers...*

It is as if Paul is trying to wake the church up to the true battle, which was never homeland but entirely foreign. We have filled our services with great messages, each one with a focus to help us align our domestic life, which is crucial and in actual fact the purpose of the Pastor. But when churches become pastoral and not apostolic/prophetic, this domestic policy focus causes us to lose our military outlook. Family is not the end it is the means. If we are not raising family on a mission then the family will soon turn on itself, why, because families were built for warfare. The enemies primary attack on the church has been to so entangle us in domestic and arbitrary things that we major on the minor and never put a dent in darkness. If he can get us to fight on family lines, racial lines and tribal lines, then we will always wrestle flesh and blood and therefore be missing in the realm of the spirit where the true war is. This is why Paul told Timothy,

No one serving as a soldier (strateuó) gets entangled in civilian affairs, but rather tries to please his commanding officer.
1 Timothy 2:4

To enter into military service, we must relinquish our rights to be right. Be willing to lose as many battles as we can so we can win the war. The enemy has convinced many of us that we are in demonic warfare when we are still in domestic warfare. Don't make a mission out of the submission. Get your house in order so we can fight the good fight of faith and not the bad fight of flesh.

About the Author

Tomi Arayomi received the Lord Jesus at the age of 15 and began ministry at 16 years old serving as a pastor under Foundation Faith Church. He served there and planted 10+ churches on university campuses UK wide whilst studying Law at University of Hertfordshire. He was later recognised for his apostolic and prophetic anointing and commissioned under Christian International by Dr Bill Hammond and Dr Sharon Stone on the 13th November 2010 where he currently serves as one of its trustees.

Tomi has since featured on mainstream media including BBC, Revelation TV, the Times Malawi, TBN, Channels TV, where he has been recognised for his National and personal prophetic accuracy. Tomi is a governmental prophet and has had the privilege of consulting prophetically with leaders of Nations in their homes, the United Nations and Parliament where he has frequented.

Tomi Arayomi is an author of 10 compelling books and one of the Apostolic Overseers of My Church Windsor, which saw its inception in 2016 and is a thriving church community in the heart of Windsor United Kingdom.

In 2007, Tomi founded RIG Nation with the vision to restore the apostolic and prophetic ministry back into the Body of Christ and to equip this generation to be in a position and condition for use by God. RIG stands for Restoring Issachar's Generation, a mission formed by the scripture, 1 Chronicles

12:32, "Of the sons of Issachar who had an understanding of the times to know what Israel ought to do..."

For RIG Nation community app available on iOS and android: community.rignation.app

For Tomi's instagram:
www.instagram.com/tomiarayomi

For Tomi's twitter:
www.twitter.com/tomiarayomi

For Tomi's YouTube:
www.youtube.com/tomiarayomi